INTERNATIONAL Herald Tribune.

Published With The New York Times and The Washington Post

IN THE NEWS

Ethel Tiersky
Maxine Chernoff

National Textbook Company
a division of *NTC Publishing Group* • Lincolnwood, Illinois USA

W9-DAQ-519

Published by National Textbook Company, a division of NTC Publishing Group,
4255 West Touhy Avenue, Lincolnwood (Chicago), Illinois 60646-1975 U.S.A.
© 1993 NTC Publishing Group and International Herald Tribune s.a.
Manufactured in the United States of America.

3 4 5 6 7 8 9 0 VP 9 8 7 6 5 4 3 2 1

Contents

SECTION 5   97

Arts and Leisure

SECTION 6   123

Science and Environment

SECTION 7   147

Sports

COMPREHENSION CHECK   169

Introduction

To the Student

In the News: Mastering Reading and Language Skills with the Newspaper features 30 articles selected from the *International Herald Tribune,* an English-language newspaper edited in Paris, France, and distributed around the world, making it the world's only global newspaper.

We have selected articles on a wide range of interesting issues in the areas of news, science, education, sports, business, and arts and leisure. You'll read about why humans can still beat computers at chess, how Russians are coping with the change to a market economy, what is happening at Euro Disney, and many other thought-provoking topics.

As you explore the issues in the news, you will strengthen your reading skills. The exercises that accompany the articles are designed to help you better understand the articles' main points and their vocabulary and idioms. In addition, special Focus on the Newspaper activities provide a bridge from the guided reading in this text to reading and analyzing articles in daily newspapers effectively on your own.

Reading skills do not exist apart from other communication skills. Throughout this text, you will share ideas by talking and writing about the issues.

In conclusion, we hope that you enjoy reading and discussing the material in this text and in your daily English-language newspapers.

To the Teacher

In the News: Mastering Reading and Language Skills with the Newspaper is designed to help students develop competence and confidence in reading the newspaper and, at the same time, apply their reading skills to all other kinds of materials, from textbooks to popular fiction.

The newspaper is a highly effective learning tool. This text contains 30 articles on a wide range of interesting topics, taken directly from the pages of the *International Herald Tribune.* Exercises accompanying the articles provide students with the framework and the help they need to grasp key ideas and concepts and to understand and practice useful idioms and vocabulary.

Focus on the Newspaper pages, which occur at the beginning of the text and at the end of each of the seven sections, help students understand the kinds of information they can expect to find in the newspaper and give them hands-on practice in analyzing various kinds of newspaper articles. The sections are designed as a bridge to encourage students to apply the approaches and skills they are learning in this book to their independent reading.

The exercises that accompany each article follow a definite pattern to facilitate their use in the classroom. Here is an outline of their contents.

Previewing the Article

- Introduces the topic of the article and provides background information helpful in understanding the article
- Provides points for discussion to stimulate students' interest in the article and to activate students' prior knowledge about the topic
- Suggests a purpose to guide students' reading of the article

Getting the Message

- Comprehension items focus on key points; the setup allows students to confirm their understanding of the article on their own by using the Comprehension Check at the back of this text
- Some exercises focus on basic reading comprehension and critical thinking skills, such as scanning for specific information, classifying information from the article, and identifying main points

Expanding Your Vocabulary

- Asks students to determine the meaning of words through the context in which they are used
- Provides practice in defining vocabulary and using it in context

Working with Idioms

- Lists and defines key idioms and expressions from the article
- Provides contextualized practice of the idioms

Analysis of a Key Aspect of the Article

Has a variety of exercise titles to describe the specific task for the article; for example *Analyzing Style and Tone, Analyzing Paragraphs,* and *Making Sense of Sentences.* Tasks require students to analyze:

- author's implied attitude toward the subject, as expressed in style and tone
- the overall structure of the article, as well as the function and purpose of individual paragraphs
- sentence structure, for example, noun clauses, *if* clauses, use of connectors that contrast ideas, and other such sentence-level features

Talking and Writing

- provides several topics relating to issues in the articles for students to discuss or write about
- uses the article as a springboard for communicative activities

Specific suggestions for presenting each article are given in the Instructor's Manual.

FOCUS ON THE NEWSPAPER

How to Read the Newspaper for Information and Enjoyment

Overview of the Newspaper; Your Newspaper Reading Habits; Analyzing Headlines

Daily newspapers offer you a whole world to explore. Within their pages, you will find articles that inform, educate, excite, anger or concern you. By reading the newspaper, you can find out about what's happening throughout the world: locally, nationally and internationally. In this Focus, you will learn about some general features of newspapers to aid you in reading them on your own, and you will examine your current newspaper reading habits.

Overview of the Newspaper

Newspapers use a number of devices to help their readers find information they want quickly. Some of these are:

- boxes listing articles, found on the front page of the paper or of a section
- an index (sometimes on the second page)
- page titles
- headlines

Most newspapers are divided into sections, including news, business and sports. The sections come in a regular order; for example, often the sports section is last. Sometimes the newspaper will have special sections, for example, an entertainment, or arts and leisure, section on the weekend.

You will notice that articles often begin with a dateline, or the name of the place where the article was written. You'll find datelines from all over the world.

Exercise 1: The Setup of the Newspaper

A. Look at a recent issue of a newspaper. Circle some examples of the devices that help you find information.

B. Look over the newspaper you usually read. List the order of the sections.

Exercise 2: Locating What You Want to Find

Quickly find as many of the items as possible. Make use of the devices you located in exercise 1. Circle the items in the paper. In the first column below, write the page (and section) where the item is located.

	Where Found	Level
1. The weather	_____	_____
2. The score of a sports event	_____	_____
3. A story about a recent election	_____	_____
4. A dateline from a European country	_____	_____
5. A headline that includes the name of a country	_____	_____
6. Information about a cultural event	_____	_____
7. A letter to the editor	_____	_____
8. A photo with an entertainer or a sports figure	_____	_____

Exercise 3: Where Did It Happen?

Use the chart you just did in exercise 2. Classify the information by *where* it happens. In the second column, write:

- L for local
- N for National
- I for International

Your Newspaper Reading Habits

You find many different types of articles in a newspaper. News articles are typically at the front of the paper: these report current news and political events. Articles expressing opinions and taking positions on current issues are on the editorial pages. Feature articles give background information about the news and may express the viewpoint of the writer. They may be on a topic of general interest, such as an article on a science discovery or on a well-known entertainer.

When you read the newspaper, do you often read just particular kinds of articles, for example, sports ones? Or do you usually look through the entire newspaper to find what interests you? In this section, you will explore your reading habits so that you can make the best use of the newspaper.

Exercise 4: What Catches Your Interest?

First, you will get practice in one approach to looking at the newspaper. Do this: skim the entire newspaper and look for the articles that interest you. Read whatever catches your interest. On a separate sheet of paper, complete a chart like the following.

Name of Article/ Item	Type of Article or Item*	I Read the Headline Only	I Read the 1st Paragraph	I Quickly Skimmed It	I Read It Carefully

*Use these abbreviations: N = News story; F = Feature story; ED = Editorial/Opinion; LE = Letter to the editor; C = Cartoon; P = Photo; A = Advertisement; O = Other.

As you did the activity, did you find anything that really interested you that you might not have noticed if you followed your regular reading habits? Repeat exercise 4 several times as you work on this book. Do your reading habits change?

Exercise 5: Reviewing Your Newspaper Reading Habits

Think about the following questions. Write your thoughts in a notebook or discuss them with a partner.

1. Do you follow the same pattern each time you read the newspaper? For example, do you always look at the back page first?

2. What kinds of articles do you usually read: "hard" news stories? sports stories? editorials? comics? Why?

3. How familiar are you with various sections of the newspaper? Can you find what you're looking for quickly?

4. In the articles that you read completely, what motivates you to read? your interest in the subject? a catchy headline? the length?

5. What is your main purpose in reading the newspaper? Does it change?

6. What are some reasons you don't read the entire newspaper from front page to back page? lack of time? lack of interest? lack of familiarity with the topic? unfamiliar vocabulary?

7. Do you read a newspaper in your native language differently from the way you read an English-language paper? What are the differences?

8. Do you think your newspaper reading habits will be the same in six months? in a year? Would you like to change your reading habits? Why, or why not?

Analyzing Headlines

Headlines are designed to catch your eye and interest as you look through a newspaper. They typically summarize the gist of an article in a few words. Headlines help you predict the subject of an article and its main idea or viewpoint, and so they are important in helping you use the newspaper for your own purposes.

Headlines pose special problems in reading. Often short function words like *be* and *the* are left out. They often contain idioms, as well as word play or puns, because the headline writers are seeking to be clever and attract reader interest.

- *Straightforward headlines.* Many headlines make a clear direct statement about the subject of the article. For example, the headline "You Can't Learn Soccer in the Suburbs" states the opinion described and explained by the author in an article about the nature of soccer. Other headlines describe the topic by asking a question, as in "Should ID's Be Required? Dutch Agonize."

- *Word play.* If you look through the list of articles in this book, you will find one with the headline "Moscow Chefs: Where's the Beef?" The slang phrase "Where's the Beef?" can mean where is the substance, or the important part. Here it literally means "Where is the meat?" You'll learn why when you read the article.

- *Background knowledge.* The headline of one article is "The Latest Riddle of the Sphinx." This assumes that you know what a sphinx is and to what the first riddle of the sphinx refers. (Read Previewing the Article on page 139 to get answers to these questions.)

Exercise 6: Behind the Headlines

Look through a newspaper and pick out five headlines. Predict the subject of each article from the headline. Then read the article to find its subject. Were your predictions accurate?

Headline	Predicted Subject	Actual Subject

Exercise 7: Make the Headlines

For the five articles you worked with in exercise 6, write different headlines.

News

News

Article 1

Smokers Under 18 in Iowa Now Outlaws

Previewing the Article

Should teenagers be allowed to smoke? In the midwestern United States, the state of Iowa is trying a new solution to the problem of smoking by minors (those under 18). Because there is much disagreement about a new Iowa law on smoking, the article contains many opposing views gathered from interviews with health officials, police officers and teenagers themselves.

Before You Read

Before you read the article, discuss these questions.
1. If you smoke, when did you start? Would you discourage your children from smoking?
2. What are the dangers of smoking? Why do you think people continue smoking despite reports on its dangers?

As You Read

As you read, look for answers to these questions.
1. What does the state of Iowa hope to accomplish with the new law?
2. What are some problems with making people obey the law?

I. Getting the Message

After reading the article, choose the best answer for each item.

1. This article is mainly about
   a. smoking
   b. a new smoking law in Iowa
   c. teenagers

2. With the new law, the state of Iowa hopes to
   a. arrest many teenagers
   b. collect fines
   c. reduce tobacco use

Smokers Under 18 in Iowa Now Outlaws

By Don Terry
New York Times Service

DES MOINES—Young smokers beware: On Monday it became illegal in Iowa for anyone under 18 to smoke a cigarette.

If caught smoking, chewing or even possessing tobacco by the police, an underaged offender could be fined as much as $100, yanked off the street or out of the shopping mall and taken home in the backseat of a squad car.

The law is part of the state's campaign to reduce tobacco use greatly among all Iowans by 2000. The police are charged with enforcing the law, but some are skeptical. On their crowded list of priorities, the measure shares a spot with the neighbor's cat stuck in a tree.

"We're too busy to enforce a law like that," Sergeant Gail Dunn of the Des Moines Police Department said with a sigh.

5   Michael J. Coverdale of the Iowa Department of Public Health has heard the grumbling, and his terse response is, "The law is the law."

But for the first year or so, Mr. Coverdale said, he thinks the police will simply inform underaged smokers about the law and confiscate their cigarettes.

"I doubt the police would actually arrest a juvenile for smoking," he said. "But they certainly will have the option to."

Forty-four states have laws—rarely enforced—that bar selling cigarettes to minors or bar minors from possessing tobacco, said Tim Hensley of the Centers for Disease Control's office on Smoking and Health, in Atlanta.

"But I'm not aware of any other state that actually says they are prohibited from smoking," he said.

10   The grown-ups in Des Moines say the new law is for the "kids' own good," because, after all, Mr. Coverdale said, "cigarettes are often a gateway to other drugs that are illegal."

The kids are not so sure.

"It's stupid," declared Wendi Spuehler, 17, who smokes a half-pack of cigarettes a day. "I'm supposed to be an American. I'm supposed to be able to do whatever I want. If I choose to ruin my lungs, it's my choice and not the cops'."

Some police officers in Iowa are not too keen about the law, either.

In Davenport, Lieutenant Michael C. Hammes said he doubted that the measure would "scare very many kids" away from cigarettes.

15   "I started smoking when I was 13," he said. "My parents didn't scare me from smoking. And I feared my father more than I feared the police, and he couldn't stop me."

The tobacco industry, which has been under attack in the courts over liability in smokers' deaths, has no argument with the law. Even the Tobacco Institute, an industry lobby group in Washington, supports it.

---

3. Unlike laws in other states in the United States, the Iowa law
    a. bars the selling of cigarettes to minors
    b. bars police from arresting minors for smoking
    c. prohibits minors from smoking

4. Some officials worry that the new law
    a. cannot be enforced
    b. will cause many teenagers to become violent
    c. will result in many teenagers going to jail

5. Similar laws against smoking in other states
    a. are very effective
    b. are rarely enforced
    c. reduce the death rate from smoking

Check your answers with the key on page 169. If you have made mistakes, reread the article to gain a better understanding of it.

▬ II. Expanding Your Vocabulary

Getting Meaning from Context

Use context clues to determine the meaning of each word, found in the paragraph indicated in parentheses. Choose the correct definition.

1. beware (1):   a. be on guard against   b. be good
2. skeptical (3):   a. believing   b. doubtful
3. charged (3):   a. attacked   b. responsible for
4. measure (3):   a. ruler   b. law
5. confiscate (6):   a. take away   b. use
6. possessing (8):   a. owning   b. knowing
7. prohibited (9):   a. forbidden   b. allowed
8. liability (16):   a. legal responsibility   b. choice
9. lobby (16):   a. a group of people engaged b. a large public area inside
                             in influencing lawmakers   a building

▬ III. Working with Idioms

Study the meanings of these idioms and expressions.

caught smoking (2) = found inhaling a cigarette

share a spot with (3) = be considered the same

have the option to (7) = to be able to choose to

not too keen about (13) = not very enthusiastic about

Answer these questions.

1. In paragraph 2, who can be *caught smoking* and who will do the catching?
2. In paragraph 3, why does the new law *share a spot with* the police handling a neighbor's cat being stuck in a tree?
3. In paragraph 7, will most police who *have the option to* arrest teens do so?
4. In paragraph 13, why are the police *not too keen about* the law?

▬ IV. Analyzing Paragraphs

Because there is so much disagreement about the effects of the new smoking law, the article quotes many different opinions on the subject. Each opinion is presented in a direct quotation. Go back through the paragraphs containing direct quotations. Complete the chart, telling whether the person being quoted is for or against the new law and why. Choose three quotations.

Para.	Speaker's Name/Job	For or Against	Reason(s)
4	Gail Dunn/police officer	against	"too busy to enforce"

Now ask a few classmates about their opinion of the law. Introduce each student by name and occupation. Then write the student's opinion, using a sentence or sentences in a direct quotation.

Example: Frank Wong is a student. He says, "The law is not fair to young people. They have the right to choose to smoke or not."

V. Talking and Writing

Discuss the following topics. Then choose one of them to write about.

1. Crimes can be divided into two categories: (1) those involving victims such as robbery and kidnapping and (2) victimless crimes such as the use of illegal substances. Are there laws in your society against both types of crime? Should protecting people from harming themselves be the role of government?

2. What is your opinion of the new Iowa law? Should minors be prohibited by law from smoking?

News

Should ID's Be Required? Dutch Agonize

Previewing the Article

Do you sometimes feel that you are just a number? Many people object to the idea of being thought of as a number instead of a person. But more important to some is the fear of having their actions monitored by means of their "number." Nonetheless, does society have the legitimate need to keep track of its citizens for the good of the whole? And does a national identity card meet this need?

These are issues that the Dutch are currently "agonizing" over—that is, worrying about and debating. The article describes this debate.

Before You Read

Before you read the article, discuss these questions.
1. Does your native country have a national identity card? If so, do you object to carrying one, or do you find it useful?

2. What kinds of identification do you carry? What purposes do they serve?

As You Read

As you read, find reasons for and against the national ID card in the Netherlands.

I. Getting the Message

After reading the article, choose the best answer for each item.

1. In the past, the Netherlands rejected an ID card because
   a. the cost was too high for the government
   b. it was against people's individual freedoms
   c. a European card was in use

2. All European Community (EC) countries have ID cards
   a. except for the Netherlands
   b. except for the Netherlands and three other countries
   c. except for the Netherlands and Britain

3. One major use for the ID card in the Netherlands would be to
   a. check people selling on the street
   b. keep statistics on people who use public transportation
   c. check people applying for jobs

Should ID's Be Required? Dutch Agonize

By Jeffrey Stalk
Special to the Herald Tribune

AMSTERDAM—The French have one. So do the Germans and the Belgians. And for years the Dutch have wrestled with the question of whether they, too, should issue a national identity card.

The idea of making it compulsory for adults to carry such a document has been rejected in the Netherlands as incompatible with the country's traditional democratic values.

But a growing number of legislators, citing economic, judicial and political reasons, see a need to adopt some sort of plan for a compulsory identity document.

One reason, officials say, centers on making a "borderless Europe" viable. If the European Community goes ahead with plans to abolish border controls and obviate the need for passports to travel within the member nations, other means have to be found to learn who is in the Netherlands legally.
5 The Dutch center-left coalition government has ruled out proposals for a national identity card.

"We don't want a situation here that has happened elsewhere in Europe where the police arbitrarily stop people on the street and ask to see their identity card," said a spokesman for the Justice Ministry. "It leads to discrimination."

Britain, Denmark and Ireland are the only other EC member states that do not have identity cards.

The Dutch government is working on a plan for a limited form of obligatory identification. Under a law being prepared, identification would have to be carried in certain situations, such as when applying for a job.

The law would give the police the power to detain suspects briefly if they failed to identify themselves.
10 The absence of any mandatory identification has created a headache for law enforcement agencies. One major nuisance has been people who use public transportation without paying the fare. In Amsterdam alone, it is estimated that the 1990 loss from this was 10 million guilders (about $5.8 million).

Under present law, someone caught riding a bus or subway without a ticket can be taken to the police station. But if the violator refuses to provide identification, officers have little choice but to release him or her. The same happens with people arrested on a variety of misdemeanor charges, including disturbing the peace at sports events.

A more serious problem has been the people who "work black," that is, who do not report earnings to the tax authorities. The figure is believed to be considerable, both for legal and illegal residents.

Between 20,000 and 100,000 people are believed to be living and, in many cases, working illegally in the Netherlands. With the fall of communism in the former Soviet bloc and the outbreak of warfare in the republics that made up Yugoslavia, the number of illegal residents has swelled. Officials estimate that 6 billion guilders were lost in tax revenue last year through unreported income.

The government briefly considered a proposal making it compulsory for all employees to buy a special identity card. But the Labor Party, the minority coalition partner, objected to the cost.
15 Nearly everybody in the work force has a driver's license, said Danielle Cardozo, the Labor spokeswoman, so the government decided a driver's license was sufficient.

The plan for compulsory identification suffered a setback this week when the Council of State, an advisory body, judged that such a law would discriminate against foreigners and citizens of foreign origin.

But Justice Minister Ernst Hirsch Ballin said the law would establish tight controls on when a person must show identification.

---

4. Some argue that one positive effect of a national ID could be
    a. more money collected in taxes
    b. less crime
    c. more respect for the law

5. One negative effect could be
    a. high costs
    b. fewer jobs
    c. discrimination against foreigners

Check your answers with the key on page 169. If you have made mistakes, reread the article to gain a better understanding of it.

II. Expanding Your Vocabulary

A. Getting Meaning from Context

Use context clues to determine the meaning of each word, found in the paragraph indicated in parentheses. Choose the correct definition.

1. wrestled (1):   a. fought intensely   b. tried to decide on a difficult issue

2. citing (3):   a. giving as an explanation for   b. deciding on a place for

3. adopt (3):   a. approve officially   b. change to suit one's needs

4. viable (4):   a. workable   b. competitive

5. obviate (4):   a. establish   b. eliminate

6. discrimination (6): a. good judgment   b. difference in treatment of a group of people in society

7. mandatory (10):   a. organized   b. required

8. swelled (13):   a. greatly increased in size   b. slightly increased in size

B. Reading for Suggested Meanings

Answer the questions.

1. In paragraph 2, a national ID is said to be *incompatible* with the country's democratic tradition.
   a. Does that mean that it fits in with the tradition or that it doesn't?
   b. How can an ID be incompatible with democracy?

2. In paragraph 6, a spokesman says that the country wants to avoid situations where police can *arbitrarily* stop people on the street. What does *arbitrarily* suggest about how the police could select people to stop and question?

3. In paragraph 17, what kind of controls are *tight* controls? Would people who are concerned with individual rights want tight controls?

III. Working with Idioms

Study the meanings of these idioms and expressions.

go ahead with (4) = continue with

rule out (5) = eliminate, end

create a headache (10) = create a problem

suffer a setback (16) = have something happen to stop one's progress

Complete the sentences with the idioms and expressions.

1. The current Dutch government has _____ proposing a national ID card, although some people in politics see the need for one.

2. The supporters of the national ID card _____ in their efforts when a court ruled against a law making work identification cards necessary.

3. The European Community wants to _____ plans to eliminate "borders" between its members.

4. Not being able to identify people can _____ for police.

IV. Analyzing Paragraphs

The news article describes an issue, presenting both sides. Several of the paragraphs in the article are used to describe the various positions in the debate.

1. One argument against the national ID card is presented in paragraph 6. What is the argument?

2. One argument for the national ID card is presented in paragraph 12. What is the argument?

3. Do paragraphs 10 and 11 present a positive or negative argument? What is it?

V. Talking and Writing

Discuss the following topics. Then choose one of them to write about.

1. What negative effects can a national ID card have? What are its possible positive effects? What is your own personal position?

2. Is there any law being proposed in the country where you live that has caused debate? What is it? What are the positions in the debate? What side do you take?

News

Article 3

EC Sets 'Ecolabel' for Green Products

Previewing the Article

Can government, industry and consumers work together to improve the environment? It's been tried before with some success. Now the European Community (EC) has created a new symbol called the ecolabel, which is to be awarded to products that are "friendly" to the environment. Some of the EC's 12 member nations are already doing something similar on a national level, but the marketing reach of the EC should make its ecolabel far more influential than any national symbol.

The following article deals mostly with the ecolabel, but the last three paragraphs take up another recent EC effort, the attempt to create a fund to fight against air pollution.

Before You Read

Before you read the article, do the following:
1. Look at the illustration of the new ecolabel that accompanies the article. What do you think these symbols stand for: the flower, the E and the 12 stars?
2. Discuss the meaning of the phrase "green products."
3. Discuss "green" parties. What kinds of actions do they support?

As You Read

As you read, look for reasons why the ecolabel is likely to be more effective than 12 different ecology awards given by individual EC member nations.

I. Getting the Message

After reading the article, indicate if each item is true (*T*) or false (*F*).

_____ 1. The EC ecolabel system will simplify the process of buying environmentally safe products and make it more reliable.

_____ 2. The EC determines the criteria for receiving an ecolabel.

_____ 3. Even if a product is produced in an ecologically safe way, it does not qualify for an ecolabel if it harms the environment when discarded.

EC Sets 'Ecolabel' for Green Products

By Charles Goldsmith
International Herald Tribune

BRUSSELS—A flower whose petals form 12 stars encircling an "E" will soon become a familiar sight on European Community products from washing machines to paints.

EC environment ministers on Thursday adopted a new system to award an "ecolabel" to products deemed friendly to the environment, and manufacturers are expected to aggressively seek the new seal of approval.

"For the first time, consumers throughout the EC will be able to get reliable guidance to help them choose the products that do least damage to the environment," said the British environment minister, David Trippier.

Officials felt that a Community-wide ecolabel based on clearly defined environmental standards was necessary to prevent consumers from being misled by spurious claims of ecological benevolence or confused by a plethora of national green labels.

5   Germany's Blue Angel environmental label has been awarded for two decades, and several other EC countries have planned to implement their own programs.

Under the wholly voluntary EC program, criteria for the green label will be set by a panel of specialists from industry, retail trades and the environmental and consumer movements. National authorities will then decide whether a given product qualifies, based on a cradle-to-grave assessment of an item's production, use and disposal.

Manufacturers said an EC-wide system will help consumers as well as industry.

"It's very clearly better to have one label rather than several," said David Veitch, European spokesman for

Procter & Gamble Co., the U.S.-based consumer products company. "We market products on a European basis, so a single ecolabel holds many advantages in terms of costs and focusing our efforts to develop better products."

He cautioned, however, that it would be "very difficult" to establish workable criteria for some products, such as laundry detergent, because there are many factors to consider, including biodegradability, water consumption and packaging.

10   The environment ministers are to be joined on Friday by national energy ministers to debate the EC Commission's controversial plan for an energy tax to combat carbon dioxide emissions.

The ministers are expected to tell the Commission that they need more detailed information on the side effects of such a tax before they could consider any formal legislative proposal. The Commission's plans were outlined in September as an informal "communication" to national governments.

Only Germany, Denmark and the Netherlands want the Commission to issue a formal proposal at this time.

_____   4.   The 12 stars in the ecolabel probably symbolize the 12 months of the year.

_____   5.   Manufacturers will want to earn ecolabels because they will attract customers.

_____   6.   In order to earn an ecolabel, some manufacturers may make changes in their products.

_____   7.   In the EC member nations, the only products that can be sold are those that qualify for an ecolabel.

Check your answers with the key on page 169. If you have made mistakes, reread the article to gain a better understanding of it.

II. Expanding Your Vocabulary

A. Getting Meaning from Context

Use context clues to determine the meaning of each word or phrase, found
in the paragraph(s) indicated in parentheses. Choose the correct definition.

1. deemed (2):   a. judged to be   b. trying to be
2. standards (4):   a. bases for comparison and   b. limitations on use
                                judging
3. clearly (4, 8):   a. obviously; easily seen   b. possibly
                                and understood
4. consumer movements (6):   a. groups of customers   b. organizations working to
                                dedicated to introducing   protect consumers'
                                new products   interests
5. criteria (6, 9):   a. detailed designs   b. rules or principles for
                                                                     evaluating something
6. panel (6):   a. a group of people   b. a piece of wood
7. qualifies (6):   a. is of high quality   b. has the requirements for
8. assessment (6):   a. tax   b. evaluation

B. Matching Opposites

Match each word with its opposite.

1. benevolence   _____ required
2. consumer   _____ decide not to do
3. implement   _____ honest, truthful
4. plethora   _____ partly
5. spurious   _____ harm, damage
6. voluntary   _____ very few of
7. wholly   _____ manufacturer

C. Practicing Useful Vocabulary

Complete these sentences with words from exercise B.

1. The EC plans to _____ a new policy for labeling products.
2. The ecolabel helps the _____ know that the products with the symbol are
   ecologically safe; the individual won't be misled by _____ claims of product safety
   from manufacturers.
3. The new ecolabel replaces a _____ of labels with one standard label.

III. Making Sense of Sentences

A clause beginning with *whose* is an adjective clause that expresses either ownership or a relationship of belonging.

Example: The company *whose* product meets certain criteria may put a special label on it.

(*Whose* relates the words *company* and *product*: the product was made by the company.)

The article begins with a sentence containing an adjective clause with *whose*. Find the sentence. What two things are being related?

Now complete these five sentences using information you learned from the article. Each sentence contains a *whose* clause.

1. Companies whose ecological claims are false _____.

2. A manufacturer whose products are ecologically friendly _____.

3. A consumer whose washing machine is too old to fix _____.

4. A spokesman whose _____ said that a single ecolabel has many advantages.

5. A product whose _____ is not likely to earn an ecolabel.

IV. Talking and Writing

Discuss the following topics. Then choose one of them to write about.

1. Ecological considerations may affect your behavior as a consumer. What labels do you look for when you make purchases? If a product is made with recycled paper or biodegradable packaging, are you more likely to buy it?

2. People active in the ecology movement urge everyone to conserve energy. What are some ways to do this? What do you do to try to conserve energy?

3. Do you think the new ecolabel will affect how products are manufactured and which products people buy? Why, or why not?

News

Article 4

A Rain of Protest on Columbus's Parade

Previewing the Article

On October 12th of each year, many people in the United States celebrate the anniversary of the discovery of America. Although Columbus sailed his ships under a Spanish flag, he was Italian, and Italian-Americans have always taken great pride in Columbus. They have celebrated Columbus Day as their "ethnic holiday" with parades and dinners. Not all people, however, are quite as happy about the holiday.

"Don't rain on my parade," one person tells another, meaning "don't ruin my happy occasion." The rain on the annual Columbus Day celebration is in the form of political protest. In 1992, with the 500th anniversary of Columbus's "discovery" of America, there was heated debate over the meaning of his voyage. Some American Indian groups claim that his "discovery" was an invasion. How to reconcile the conflict over the holiday in the United States, a land of diversity, is discussed in this news article.

Before You Read

Before you read the article, discuss these questions.
1. Is there a holiday for an important historical figure in your native country? What did this person achieve? How is the holiday celebrated?
2. Is there controversy over any holiday celebrated in your country? Is there any new holiday that people are trying to introduce?

As You Read

As you read, look for reasons for which American Indian groups in the United States protest the celebration of Columbus Day.

© Esbin-Anderson Photography

In the United States, parades on October 12, Columbus Day, have traditionally commemorated Columbus's arrival in the New World.

A Rain of Protest on Columbus's Parade

To American Indians, the Holiday Celebrates an Invasion, Not a Discovery

By Dirk Johnson
New York Times Service

DENVER—Will Rogers, who was part American Indian, once remarked that while his ancestors did not come over on the Mayflower, "they were there to greet the boat."

The comedian used humor to state the obvious: that civilization on the North American continent hardly began with the arrival of Europeans. But if it is so obvious, many American Indians ask, what is all this hoopla surrounding Christopher Columbus?

In Denver, and around the United States as celebrations are planned to mark the 500th anniversary of Columbus's arrival, American Indian groups are planning their own observances— but in protests, not parades. To them, the national holiday marks an invasion, not a discovery.

To the consternation of Italian-American groups here, members of the American Indian Movement, a leading Indian advocacy group, are demanding the removal of a plaque at the civic center that commemorates Co-

lumbus as "Discoverer of America."

5   In a letter to Mayor Wellington Webb, who is black, the group wrote: "As an African-American, we hope that you can empathize with our feelings on this matter. It would be as if the city had a statue honoring slave traders or the Ku Klux Klan."

There were Indian protests and spiritual ceremonies to coincide with Columbus Day parades around the country this weekend. Native American spiritual leaders and supporters gathered at the Capitol Mall in Washington on Monday, and American Indian groups in other cities planned sunrise ceremonies.

"For us, Columbus was no hero," said Suzan Shown Harjo, a spokeswoman in Washington for the 1992 Alliance, a consortium of American Indian groups formed to oppose the Columbus holiday. "For us, Western civilization was no gift. We urge all people of conscience to forgo celebration of five centuries of genocide. We urge all to listen to our voices and to join us now to make the next 500 years different from the past 500 years."

On Saturday, about 50 Indians briefly blocked a Columbus Day parade in Denver, beating drums and chanting, "No parades for murderers."

Denver's human relations commissioner, Steven L. Newman, said the city was trying to settle the dispute over the Columbus plaque. The Italian-American groups have made it plain that they oppose its removal, while Indian groups reject any official tribute to Columbus. The rift has been exacerbated by vows from members of the Ku Klux Klan to protect the Columbus plaque.

10 Mr. Newman said: "There has to be a way to show appreciation for both groups, the Italian-Americans and the Native Americans. We need to find a way to get there."

But history cannot be compromised, said John Emhoolah, the acting director of the Denver Indian Center. He rejected the idea that Columbus deserves any recognition. "He was a visitor, that's all," Mr. Emhoolah said. "As a child, I remember the elders telling us that our people had been here a long, long time. They had many legends to tell. But they never mentioned this guy Columbus."

Italian-Americans here say they fear they have been made a scapegoat. Frank Busnardo, the president of the Federation of Italian-American Organizations in Denver, which sponsored a Columbus Day parade on Saturday, said Columbus Day should honor all people. He said his group would reject any "assistance" from the Klan or other racist groups.

"The theme for our parade is that Columbus is a bridge between two worlds—the Old World and the New World," Mr. Busnardo said. "The Italian community has gotten a bad deal out of this. It's supposed to be for all ethnic groups, including the Indians."

But Mr. Emhoolah said that joining the Columbus celebrations would be a betrayal.

15 "We're getting to the last of the people who know the language, the culture," he said. "I don't know what it's going to be like in 2091. I don't know if there will be any tribes. I hope so. It's our responsibility to pass on the culture to the next generation.

"When it comes to Christopher Columbus, we can't pay too much attention to that. I know the Europeans think the world of him. But that's their deal. It's not mine."

I. Getting the Message

After reading the article, choose the best answer for each item.

1. Civilization in North America clearly began
    a. with Columbus's arrival
    b. before Columbus's arrival
    c. with the Mayflower's arrival

2. The issue that the article describes is whether or not
    a. an American citizen has the right to demonstrate
    b. parades are the best way to celebrate Columbus Day
    c. Columbus Day should be celebrated

3. Indian groups in Denver wish to
    a. erect a statue to slavery
    b. celebrate Columbus's birthday
    c. remove a plaque that honors Columbus's "discovery"

4. The opinion of Italian-American groups toward Columbus Day is that it
    a. is supposed to honor all ethnic groups
    b. will have to be eliminated because of the Indian protests
    c. should be celebrated along with a new holiday to honor American Indians

5. According to the article, many American Indians feel that Columbus was
    a. a person with no effect on the American Indians
    b. an invader of North America
    c. a hero

Check your answers with the key on page 169. If you have made mistakes, reread the article to gain a better understanding of it.

II. Expanding Your Vocabulary

Getting Meaning from Context

Use context clues to determine the meaning of each word, found in the paragraph indicated in parentheses. Choose the correct definition.

1. ancestors (1):
   a. children
   b. parents, grandparents, and so on

2. surrounding (2):
   a. environment
   b. connected with

3. observances (3):
   a. ceremonies
   b. acts of watching

4. empathize (5):
   a. understand someone else's feelings
   b. disagree with someone else's position

5. forgo (7):
   a. come before
   b. do without

6. genocide (7):
   a. disrespect and hatred
   b. planned killing of a race

7. vows (9):
   a. promises
   b. speeches

8. appreciation (10):
   a. gratitude
   b. increase in value

9. betrayal (14):
   a. a moment of anger
   b. an act of disloyalty

III. Working with Idioms

Study the meanings of these idioms and expressions.

rain on a parade (headline) = ruin a happy event

hoopla (2) = commotion or excitement

find a way to get there (10) = solve a problem

make a scapegoat (12) = turn into a victim

get a bad deal (13) = be treated poorly

pass on to (15) = go from one to another

think the world of (16) = have a very good opinion of

Study these names from the article.

Will Rogers (1) = U.S. comedian (1879-1935) known for his satirical political comments

Mayflower (1) = a ship on which settlers sailed to found the first permanent English settlement in what is now the United States

Ku Klux Klan (5, 9, 12) = an organization noted as opposing African-Americans with violence

Answer these questions.

1. In paragraph 2, why don't the American Indians wish to participate in the *hoopla*?

2. In paragraph 13, why have the Italian-Americans *gotten a bad deal*?

3. In paragraph 15, what do the American Indians want to *pass on to* the next generation?

4. In paragraph 16, according to the Indian spokesman, the Europeans *think the world of* Columbus. Do the American Indians?

IV. Focusing on Style and Tone

Because the article discusses the conflict over Columbus Day, both negative and positive words are used to describe the same person or event. For example, in the title *discovery* is a positive description of Columbus's arrival; *invasion* is a negative one. Place the following words into their proper categories: hero, honor, genocide, tribute, scapegoat, discoverer, hoopla, betrayal.

Positive	Negative

Can you think of sets of words that have both positive and negative connotations (suggested meanings)? Here's an example: *student* (neutral), *scholar* (positive), *bookworm* (negative). Think of your own examples.

V. Talking and Writing

Discuss the following topics. Then choose one of them to write about.

1. Is there a controversial figure in the history of your native country? Why is there a difference of opinion about this person?

2. Choose your side in the Columbus Day controversy, and using information from this article, express your feelings about the holiday in the voice of an American Indian or an advocate of the holiday. Use the first-person (*I*).

FOCUS ON THE NEWSPAPER

News

Skimming News Articles; Analyzing News Articles

Most people read a daily newspaper to find out what is happening in their community, their city, their country and around the globe. Newspapers have daily headlines and accompanying articles about the most important events affecting our lives. Whether it's a development in international or national politics, the success of a space mission or the result of an important election, the news pages present the important facts on the subject.

Hard News Articles

Typically the "hard" news stories are on the front pages of newspapers. Hard or pure news stories report basic facts about an event or situation. Here are some essential characteristics that distinguish pure news articles:

- They report the facts, usually without giving the writer's viewpoint.
- They are usually short and to the point.
- They are organized to give all the important information in the first few paragraphs.

With a news article, you can usually answer the important questions—*who, what, where, when* and sometimes *why* or *how*—very quickly by reading the first few paragraphs. These are called the five "W" questions. The first few paragraphs are called the lead paragraphs. News articles are typically written in a standard format in which there are lead paragraphs. If you want more detail and elaboration, the rest of the article provides further information.

Exercise 1: Skimming a News Article

Choose a news article from a recent newspaper. Read the headline and read the first few paragraphs. Then answer these questions.

1. *Who* or *what* is the article about?
2. *Where* did the events take place?
3. *When* did the events take place?

Now skim (read quickly) the rest of the article.

4. What additional facts did you learn about the subject?
5. If you hadn't looked at the rest of the article, what information would you have missed?
6. Usually your past knowledge about a topic in the news helps you understand the article. What past knowledge did you have about the topic that helped you understand it?

A Closer Look at News Articles

Analyzing a news article can help you become a more critical reader of the newspaper. Consider: Why is a topic in the newspaper at this time? If the topic is controversial, are both sides of an issue fairly represented?

Exercise 2: The News in Depth

Choose a new article to analyze. Answer these questions.

Analyzing a News Article

1. Does the article cover the five ''W'' questions in the first few paragraphs? Briefly tell *who* or *what*, *where, when* and *why* or *how*. _____ _____ _____

2. What did you know about the subject before you read the article? _____

3. What did you learn by reading the article? _____

4. If there is a photo with the article, how does the photo support the main idea of the article? _____ _____

   If the article does not have a photo, imagine that you are a photo editor and indicate a subject for a photo to accompany the article. _____ _____

5. Is there any slant or bias in the article, for example, in the selection of the facts? Does the information on the news event differ from what you heard on the radio, saw on television or read in another newspaper? _____ _____

6. Imagine that you are the editor who assigns news stories. Assign a reporter to do a follow-up feature article on some aspect of the article. Explain to the reporter what you believe the focus of the article should be. _____ _____

7. Is there anything in the article that is controversial? What is it? _____ _____

8. Imagine that you are the editor of the opinion page. Assign an editorial topic to a writer. The topic should take a position on what is reported in the article. Explain to the reporter what the focus of the editorial should be. _____ _____

Opinion

Opinion

You Can't Learn Soccer in the Suburbs

Previewing the Article

In the article, it is the opinion of a British journalist stationed in the suburbs of Washington, D.C., that soccer is not properly appreciated in the United States. What soccer represents to him is a truly democratic game, played on the streets of working-class communities all over the world. Are the lush lawns and stadiums of the suburbs the proper place for a child to learn the game?

Before You Read

Before you read this article, answer the following questions.
1. Is soccer "the world's most democratic game"? Why, or why not?
2. The author discusses the role of cable TV in televising soccer in the United States. These are privately run TV stations that users have to pay for. Are there cable stations where you live? In what type of programming do they specialize?

As You Read

As you read, look for the author's answers to these questions.
1. Why is soccer an easy game to play and understand?
2. In what ways can someone learn to appreciate soccer?

You Can't Learn Soccer in the Suburbs

By Michael Elliot

WASHINGTON—We're finally getting cable television. No choice. The cable company may be bloodsuckers incarnate, but since the U.S. networks refuse to carry anything from the world's greatest sporting event—soccer's World Cup—right-thinking people everywhere are raising a glass to Ted Turner, global visionary, man of the decade, whose TNT service is broadcasting the competition.

Every non-American has a sticking point in his praise of the United States. For myself, I can argue persuasively that American primary education is a triumph, that the contras were saints, that Eastern Airlines often takes off on time. What I absolutely cannot do is excuse or explain America's indifference to professional soccer.

America is the world's greatest democracy, and soccer is the world's most democratic game. You need no fancy equipment, no bats, no shoulder pads. You hardly need a ball (I've seen kids on Caribbean islands play with a tightly wound bunch of rags). It's the game most easy to understand. It has only one specialist position (goal-keeper), only one moderately complex rule (offside). You don't need to be big, strong, tall or even particularly fast.

Perhaps America's indifference to soccer is part of a general puzzlement about "abroad." Watching a country's soccer team is the quickest way to get a fix on what makes a society tick. Holland's great teams of the 1970s looked as if they'd stumbled out of a dope-ridden dive in Amsterdam, and probably had. Keen observers knew that perestroika was on the way when they saw the exciting Russian team of the early 1980s. Brazil's determination to be another dreary great power has been marked by a calamitous decline in the quality of its side. The Brazilians used to practice by doing an hour's samba; now they look as if they read stockbrokers' circulars.

5   American soccer-lovers will of course protest that millions of their stubborn kids play the game every weekend

AP/WIDE WORLD PHOTOS

Millions of fans worldwide avidly watch soccer events such as the World Cup, but the sport has yet to really catch on in the United States.

and that, for the first time since 1950, a fresh-faced team is representing the United States in the World Cup. Pshaw! You can't learn soccer in the suburbs; you shouldn't really play on a field until your teens. Soccer is *the* city game, meant to be played by snotty-nosed kids dodging cars in Glasgow and Liverpool, Naples and São Paolo. Bethesda, Maryland, doesn't make it.

Nobody—not a writer, not a hype-laden TV commentator—can help you love soccer. You have to do it yourself. It helps if you're raised with love for the game in your bones—my dad was born on the street next to Liverpool Football Club's stadium, my mum born two

blocks away—but this is not essential. A modicum of American open-mindedness, an appreciation of beauty, and a subscription to TNT are all that's required. Then you'll understand why, when the Elliott grandchildren ask me if I ever saw Gorbachev, I'll say "Yes—but I saw Hungary destroy Brazil in '66, I saw Ricky Villa's goal in '81; I saw Platini; I saw Pelé . . ." And—even if *you* don't—they will know exactly what I mean.

The writer is the Washington bureau chief of the Economist of London, and his money is on Holland. He contributed this comment to The Washington Post.

I. Getting the Message

After reading the article, choose the best answer for each item.

1. According to the author, you can't learn soccer in the suburbs because
   a. there are no proper facilities
   b. there is not enough interest in the game
   c. soccer is a city game

2. In the author's opinion, if one doesn't play soccer as a child in a city, a person
   a. will never love soccer
   b. can learn to play as an adult
   c. can learn to appreciate the game by watching it on television

3. In the author's opinion, soccer is the most democratic game because it is
   a. the oldest game
   b. the easiest to play and understand
   c. suitable to be played on the streets

4. The one specialist position in soccer is
   a. goalkeeper
   b. offside
   c. samba

5. The author has recently subscribed to cable television because
   a. he respects Ted Turner
   b. U.S. "free" networks refuse to carry soccer
   c. the Liverpool Football Club was playing in the World Cup

Check your answers with the key on page 169. If you have made mistakes, reread the article to gain a better understanding of it.

II. Expanding Your Vocabulary

Getting Meaning from Context

Use context clues to determine the meaning of each word, found in the paragraph indicated in parentheses. Choose the correct definition.

1. right-thinking (1):   a. conservative   b. with correct opinions
2. visionary (1):   a. person who can predict   b. person with good
                            what will happen   eyesight
3. argue (2):   a. give reasons for   b. fight against
4. excuse (2):   a. pardon or forgive   b. give permission to
5. indifference (4):   a. similarity   b. lack of concern
6. stumbled (4):   a. found by chance   b. tripped and almost fell
7. dodging (5):   a. tricking   b. moving around quickly
8. subscription (6):   a. interest in   b. agreement to pay to use
                                                        services

III. Working with Idioms

Study the meanings of these idioms and expressions.

bloodsucker incarnate (1) = someone who takes the blood, or life, out of others; in this case, who takes people's money

raising a glass (1) = drinking to salute or thank someone

sticking point (2) = any issue that causes a problem

get a fix on (4) = understand

what makes something tick (4) = how something works

be marked by (4) = be shown or indicated by

hype-laden (6) = full of exaggeration

in your bones (6) = important from the beginning, essential part

Answer these questions.

1. In paragraph 1, why should people *raise a glass to* Ted Turner?
2. In paragraph 2, what is the author's *sticking point* in praising the United States?
3. In paragraph 4, how does watching soccer make a person understand what *makes* a society *tick*?
4. In paragraph 6, why does the author have love for the game of soccer *in his bones*?

IV. Analyzing Paragraphs

Because this article makes an argument about soccer in the United States, the author is aware that not all readers will agree with him. Therefore, he needs to consider the audience reaction to his comments.

1. Paragraph 5 is a typical rebuttal paragraph. It presents opposing arguments to the author's own view. What are the two opposing arguments that American soccer lovers will offer?
2. What is the author's response to these arguments?

V. Talking and Writing

Discuss the following topics. Then choose one of them to write about.

1. The author, a devoted soccer fan, is very critical of the attitude toward soccer in the United States. Do you believe that his criticism is fair? Why, or why not?
2. Do you believe, as the author does, that watching a country's national team can explain that society to an observer? Could other aspects of the culture such as its dance, music or food do the same? Discuss some aspect of your native culture that could explain it to outsiders.

Opinion

An Economics Lesson at the Barbershop

Previewing the Article

An American writer living in Japan offers his opinion of Japanese business success. He finds the best example of this success in a very simple and unexpected setting, a husband-and-wife-owned barbershop that spares no energy in serving its customers.

Before You Read

Before you read the article, answer these questions.
1. When you go to a barbershop or beautician, what is more important to you, speed or craftsmanship?
2. Why might a barbershop that specializes in offering a relaxing atmosphere be especially popular in Japan?

As You Read

In the article, you will find many terms that relate to barbers and shaving. However, you should be able to understand the article without understanding all the specialized language. On a second reading, you may want to look up words you don't understand.

As you read, look for the economics lesson to be learned from Mr. Tanaka's barbershop.

I. Getting the Message

After reading the article, choose the best answer for each item.

1. An attention to detail has made "Japan Inc."
   a. a good place for tourists
   b. a land of many barbershops
   c. a prosperous economic power

2. In Japanese barbershops, barbers
   a. rush customers out
   b. never talk about politics
   c. talk with customers and work leisurely

An Economics Lesson at the Barbershop

By Tripp Strauss

TOKYO—In Japan, some people play golf on weekends and some form long lines in the Ginza district to watch first-run foreign films. A knowing few go to the barbershop.

A trip to a Japanese barbershop is an odyssey into the country's economic miracle, a glimpse at the same attention to detail that has made "Japan Inc." the envy of the capitalist world.

It is more than simply getting a haircut. Customers go to escape the hustle and bustle of Tokyo's frenetic pace. They go to complain about local politics and catch up on the latest neighborhood scuttlebutt.

But most of all, they go to be cranked up high in the barber's chair, to assume for at least one precious moment—regardless of their walk of life—that honorific stature uniquely revered in Japan: that of *okyakusama,* or customer.

5 So going to the barbershop here is an outing. The object is not to get it over with as quickly as possible, American-style, but to prolong the treatment and bask in its sensual pleasures.

No one understands this better than Tanaka-san, who runs a state-of-the-art barbershop just up the street from where I live, in the Minami Azabu district. Like much else in Japan, Mr. Tanaka's shop has only recently gone upscale.

Last year, he sold his small, old shop, located a few blocks from the new one, for a cool $15.3 million. With typical Japanese foresight for investing for the long pull, Mr. Tanaka plowed the proceeds into his spanking new premises.

Mr. Tanaka, 54, has been in the barbering business for 38 years. Back in 1950, he charged only 35 yen—not much compared with the 3,200 yen he receives today for a cut and shampoo. At today's exchange rates, $22 for a haircut might seem expensive, but I think it's one of the best deals in town.

You always have to wait in line at Mr. Tanaka's shop: He doesn't take reservations because he doesn't need to. But when your time comes, Mr. Tanaka directs you to the seat of honor.

10 Soon his wife is feverishly shampooing your hair, massaging your scalp with a special brush. While she scrubs, Mr. Tanaka is busy at the next chair, applying the finishing snips and snaps to another client. This tag-team approach keeps the shop running at full capacity.

Mr. Tanaka typically spends about 45 minutes cutting your hair, scrutinizing the symmetry of the sideburns with the utmost care. His cutting skills are superb, but it is in conversation that he truly excels. He knows when to talk, when to listen and when to utter the drawn-out guttural grunt of approval so common in Japanese. These insightful yet subtle dialogues with his clients create the cornerstone of Mr. Tanaka's thriving business: the repeat customer, every retailer's dream.

For the rare client not "hooked" by pleasant conversation, Mrs. Tanaka's shaving technique, with a straight-edged razor, is the showstopper. First, she places a hot towel over your face, then wipes your face with moisturizing oil.

She applies another hot towel to remove the oil and lathers you up with warm shaving cream. Finally, she methodically spends fifteen minutes shaving off every last whisker—including any stray hairs that might have found their way to your forehead or earlobes. The oil and hot-towel procedure is repeated and the reclining customer is gently coaxed into returning to earth.

Foreign businessmen trying to figure out what makes Japan's economy so successful might do well to visit a Japanese barbershop. Impeccable service isn't extra here, it's included in the price of admission.

The writer is a well barbered American stockbroker currently living in Japan. He contributed this comment to the International Herald Tribune.

---

3. Relaxation and sensual pleasure are
   a. admitted goals of customers
   b. not possible in the busy atmosphere
   c. not appreciated by hurried customers

4. Because Mr. Tanaka's shop is so popular,
   a. reservations are required
   b. people wait in line
   c. he is opening another new store

5. Not only is Mr. Tanaka a good barber, but he is also
   a. skilled at conversation
   b. an expert in shaving techniques
   c. a local politician

Check your answers with the key on page 169. If you have made mistakes, reread the article to gain a better understanding of it.

II. Expanding Your Vocabulary

Getting Meaning from Context

Use context clues to determine the meaning of each word, found in the paragraph indicated in parentheses. Choose the correct definition.

1.	revered (4):	a.	honored	b. opposed
2.	prolong (5):	a.	lengthen	b. shorten
3.	plowed (7):	a.	did farm work	b. put money back into
4.	proceeds (7):	a.	movements forward	b. money from a sale
5.	premises (7):	a.	basic ideas	b. part of a building
6.	deals (8):	a.	bargains	b. business contracts
7.	massaging (10):	a.	rubbing	b. relaxing
8.	thriving (11):	a.	very successful	b. just beginning
9.	methodically (13):	a.	carefully, according to plan	b. according to traditional methods

III. Working with Idioms

Study the meanings of these idioms and expressions.

the hustle and bustle (3) = the hurried pace

catch up on (3) = get the latest information

neighborhood scuttlebutt (3) = local gossip

get it over with (5) = finish a task

state-of-the-art (6) = modern, up-to-date

for the long pull (7) = for the future

spanking new (7) = completely new

when your time comes (9) = when it is your turn

tag-team approach (10) = approach in which members of a team keep replacing one another

the cornerstone of (11) = the basis of

Complete these sentences, using the idioms and expressions.

1. Customers can go to Mr. Tanaka's to relax and escape _____ of the crowded city. They can also _____ all the local gossip there.

2. Mr. Tanaka's new shop is _____ and _____.

3. Going to the barbershop is a leisurely experience in Japan, in contrast to the United States where customers like to _____.

4. Mr. Tanaka has many customers who come regularly. These are _____ his business.

IV. Analyzing Paragraphs

Answer these questions about the structure of the article.

1. Paragraphs 1 through 5 are the introduction of the article. What do they introduce to the reader?

2. Paragraphs 6 to 8 describe Tanaka's business and how it has changed. What are two major changes?

3. Paragraphs 9 to 13 describe what goes on in the shop. How do the Tanakas divide their duties?

4. Paragraph 14 is the conclusion. What does it suggest that foreign businesspeople can learn from a Japanese barbershop?

V. Talking and Writing

Discuss the following topics. Then choose one of them to write about.

1. If you lived in Tokyo, which activity mentioned in the story would be most satisfying to you, playing golf, sightseeing, watching a foreign film or visiting a barbershop? Why?

2. The author suggests that good customer service is the key to Japanese business success. Discuss a time when you as a customer received exceptionally good, or exceptionally poor, service.

3. In your native country, what are some services or activities for which you need a reservation or appointment? Is it different in your present hometown?

Opinion

Much Ado About Mozart: Craze Leaves Expert 'Astounded'

Previewing the Article

With the celebration of the 200th anniversary of Wolfgang Amadeus Mozart's death, the writer of this article interviews a prominent music historian, H.C. Robbins Landon, to learn whether all the "fuss" about Mozart is merely a fad. Landon contends that Mozart's rich and varied music will endure long after the movie "Amadeus" and "I love Wolfie" T-shirts are forgotten. But one thing that he can't do is fully explain why young people are so fascinated with the Mozart myth.

Before You Read

Before you read the article, discuss these questions.
1. What type of music do you enjoy? Do you listen to classical music?
2. What do you know about the life and music of Mozart?

As You Read

As you read, look for answers to these questions.
1. Why does Mozart appeal to young people?
2. What are some of the things that we don't know about Mozart?

Much Ado About Mozart: Craze Leaves Expert 'Astounded'

H.C. Robbins Landon, the music historian, has specialized in the life and work of Haydn and, more recently, Mozart. The editor of a comprehensive Mozart Dictionary, Mr. Landon spoke to Barry James of the International Herald Tribune about the bicentennial of Mozart's death, beginning in January.

Q. Is all the fuss about the Mozart anniversary justified?

A. Oh yes. There is something about Mozart that appeals in a way that no other composer in history did.

Q. He appeals a lot to young people?

A. That's right. They think he was someone who tried to fight the establishment and almost made it. They see him as a fantastic and romantic figure, chucked into a pauper's grave with five other corpses and not really understood by his contemporaries. Something else that attracts them is the fact that he was a child prodigy. They think of that little thing, aged 9, writing symphonies, which is rather amazing come to think of it. And they are quite good, too.

5   **Q.** Have you been taken by surprise by the Mozart craze?

A. Yes. I am astounded by the way the glossy magazines have latched onto Mozart. He has become the biggest myth in classical music history. The other thing which is amazing is the amount of literature which is being generated about Mozart. There is a book coming out every week. People have a mad desire to know more about him. You know, there is a classical music station in Shanghai that plays nothing but Mozart all day long. That's what people want to hear. The phenomenon is also due in part to the comeback of the 18th century. Up to now the Renaissance or the 19th century was considered much more interesting.

Q. I suppose the fact that there is so much Mozart music available also has something to do with the craze?

A. That is true. Part of Mozart's popularity is due to the compact disk. CDs are an even bigger revolution than long-playing records were. For one thing, they are ideally geared to people with small apartments. You can now buy all the works of Mozart on CD.

That means if you live in the provinces without easy reach of an orchestra, you can still have anything you want by pressing a button, and I don't think that is a bad thing.

Q. To what extent have Peter Shaffer's play "Amadeus" and the Milos Forman movie based on the play contributed to the craze?

10 A. They brought Mozart's music to thousands and thousands of families who would not otherwise have listened to it. Shaffer was very clever in writing "Amadeus." Had he tried to do a play about Bach or Haydn or Beethoven, it wouldn't have worked. But he sniffed immediately that this was going to be a huge public success, and of course when Forman did the movie, that success became magnified enormously.

Q. But "Amadeus" also created a Mozart myth?

A. Absolutely. It filled people with the idea that Mozart was a rather poor, unworthy vessel into which God in his infinite wisdom poured unlimited, fathomless amounts of great music. This, of course, is ridiculous because Mozart wasn't like that at all.

Q. What was he like?

A. He was a fanatic hard worker. He wrote the "Linz" Symphony in four or five days. Why, it would take you the whole day flat out just to copy the thing. He worked within a classical framework with supreme greatness. Haydn of course was the great innovator.

15 Q. Why hasn't there been a corresponding craze for Haydn?

A. Well, he wasn't a myth. His life was a succession of hard work and a lot of good luck, but he himself said it wasn't interesting. But as a spin-off to the Mozart phenomenon, I am doing a lot of plugging of Haydn along the route. It's curious that many people don't even want to listen to Beethoven. I was talking to some professional musicians in London, for example, and they said they hadn't played Beethoven's "Fifth" for several years.

Q. Isn't there a danger that this craze may reduce Mozart into a kind of background Muzak?

A. I don't think you really can harm Mozart very much. You cannot really do in good music, despite the "I love Wolfie" T-shirts and all the other rubbish that's going around, which you cannot prevent anyway. It is going to be very interesting to see what happens when the bicentennial is over. You know what I think? Nothing is going to happen. I think people are going to go on playing just as much Mozart as ever.

Q. Is there anything new to be said about Mozart?

20 A. There is still an awful lot we don't understand. There is not a word about the French Revolution in any of his letters, and in fact there is not a word about politics. What did he think about these things? Another thing we do not understand is why the aristocracy in Vienna stopped supporting Mozart after "Figaro" had been the success of the town. If several hundred suddenly withdrew their support, it must have been a big subject of discussion. Yet we do not have a word.

I. Getting the Message

After reading the article, choose the best answer for each item.

1. Mozart is interesting to young people because he
   a. was a romantic figure
   b. lived in the 18th century
   c. had a difficult childhood

2. The movie "Amadeus" shows
   a. what a hard worker Mozart was
   b. what a religious man Mozart was
   c. how the unworthy Mozart was gifted with music by God

3. Landon is suggesting that in terms of a composer's popularity,
   a. the myth about the composer may be more important than the composer's music
   b. the composer's music is more important than the myth about the composer
   c. we can't discover enough about a composer's life to interest us personally

4. The author believes that in the future Mozart's music will
   a. become too familiar
   b. continue to be popular
   c. lose its popularity

Check your answers with the key on page 169. If you have made mistakes, reread the article to gain a better understanding of it.

II. Expanding Your Vocabulary

A. *Getting Meaning from Context*

Use context clues to determine the meaning of each word, found in the paragraph indicated in parentheses. Choose the correct definition.

1. craze (headline):   a. insanity   b. fad

2. fuss (1):   a. a great deal of attention   b. useless worry

3. establishment (4):   a. a business   b. the group that controls society

4. contemporaries (4):   a. people living at the same time   b. people living now

5. prodigy (4):   a. talented person   b. extraordinary deed

6. framework (14):   a. system   b. platform

7. succession (16):   a. order of inheritance   b. sequence of events

8. plugging (16):   a. blocking up   b. recommending on TV or radio

9. withdrew (20):   a. took away   b. retired

B. *Practicing Useful Vocabulary*

Complete the paragraph with words from the following list. You will need to use seven of the words.

appeals	bicentennial	innovator
aristocracy	fanatic	myth
astounded	generated	phenomenon

The current popular interest in Mozart is at an all-time high. Every week more books and magazine articles are being (1) _____ about him. The huge amount of interest has (2) _____ even the music critic H.C. Robbins Landon. He thinks that the current (3) _____ is explained by the (4) _____ of Mozart, that is, the image of Mozart as a romantic figure. This image (5) _____ to young people. But Landon states that the reality of Mozart was different. Mozart was a (6) _____ at working hard. And Landon believes that the composer Haydn, not Mozart, was the great (7) _____ of the time.

III. Working with Idioms

Study the meanings of these idioms and expressions.

much ado about (headline) = a lot of fuss over and attention to

almost make it (4) = nearly succeed

latch onto (6) = associate oneself with

geared to (8) = especially designed for or suited to

easy reach of (8) = near

flat out (14) = at maximum speed or effort

spin-off (16) = something copied or developed from something else

along the route (16) = on the way

do in (18) = destroy

Answer these questions.

1. Why is there suddenly *much ado about* Mozart?
2. In paragraph 6, what have the magazines helped create by *latching onto* Mozart?
3. In paragraph 14, why would it take you the whole day *flat out* just to copy the "Linz" Symphony?
4. In paragraph 16, how is Haydn benefiting from being a *spin-off* to the Mozart craze?

IV. Focusing on Style and Tone

Since this opinion article is set up as an interview, questions alternate with responses.

1. What are three questions that the interviewer asks Mr. Landon?
2. What in addition would you like to ask Mr. Landon about Mozart? List two questions.

V. Talking and Writing

Discuss the following topics. Then choose one of them to write about.

1. If you have seen the play or movie "Amadeus," do you agree with Mr. Landon that it created a Mozart myth? Why might people be interested in this myth of Mozart rather than his true nature?
2. Have you ever met, seen or read about another prodigy? Is there a famous child prodigy from your native country? Tell about him or her.
3. Who is your favorite composer? Describe his or her music.
4. What are some other current crazes in popular culture—music, dance or fashion? Discuss a craze and give your opinion of it. Will it last?

Opinion

National Cliché or Good Metaphor?

Previewing the Article

"The mind is a computer," a professor says. This phrase is a metaphor, a type of figurative language that makes comparisons.

More than 25 years ago, an American, Martin Gannon, noticed that his new German wife did not talk at the dinner table, a habit that he later concluded was distinctly German. Observations of cultural differences like these led him to propose metaphors as a way to understand societies. He began to study how to characterize a society with a single object or tradition that best describes its nature.

The author of this article seems to suggest that Mr. Gannon's cultural comparisons are valid to some extent. However, as the title of the article, "National Cliché or Good Metaphor?" suggests, he lets the readers reach their own conclusions.

Before You Read

Before you read the article, discuss this question. Have you ever had experiences in which you were confused by the behavior of someone from another culture? What was the misunderstanding?

As You Read

As you read, look for the metaphor given for one of the societies described and the way in which Gannon explains the choice of metaphor.

National Cliché or Good Metaphor?

By Don Oldenburg
The Washington Post

WASHINGTON—Soon after his wedding 25 years ago, Martin Gannon knew something was not quite right. Every night he would watch patiently as his bride ate in virtual silence. He did not know why—not until 14 years later, when the young business professor moved his family to Kassel, Germany, to do research under a Fulbright fellowship.

His wife, Doris, then and still thoroughly American, looked forward to spending a year in the country where she was born and raised before moving to the United States at age 9.

"I found that my wife was more similar to the Germans than she was to the Americans," said Mr. Gannon, who quickly recognized his own dinner behavior to be at odds with a nation of people who see eating as a most serious business.

"I happen to be Irish-American, and the Irish really don't eat that way. Food is secondary to conversation for them."

5   If quiet meals proved to be a minor cultural clash in an otherwise harmonious marriage, they also started Martin Gannon thinking about cultural mind-sets, about how people in a society think, feel and act purely because they are members of that society.

Three years ago, after an extended stay in Bangkok, he felt he had found a way to characterize behavior in terms to promote understanding: metaphors. He fashioned a seminar to pursue such culturally potent metaphors at the University of Maryland.

Aided by graduate students, many of them foreigners, he explored ways in which to characterize diverse societies. The three-year effort has produced a 500-page manuscript whose table of contents is a collection of image-inducing entries such as the Mexican Fiesta and Belgian Lace.

Using metaphors as a serious way to describe societies is relatively new, Mr. Gannon said. He credits anthropologists with experimenting with the device, and organizational theorists with applying it in their field (the organization as "machine," for instance). To Martin Gannon, "it is the best way to cut into the culture."

To understand what "the Fatherland" is all about has little to do with the aggressiveness and rigidity often attributed to Germans. "What they really are is reflective of a symphony."

10   Not only is music a cherished part of German character and history, but Mr. Gannon contends that symphonic music symbolizes the dynamics of German society. As in a symphony orchestra, conformity is valued, order is important and rules are many, he says. And each person is expected to contribute fully his or her talents for the good of the whole.

The German education system further supports full participation by emphasizing efficiency and preparation for a place in society for everyone.

"The German," Mr. Gannon said, "sees himself as an integral part of society" and values combined effort. "If you approach German society that way, it is a lot easier" to understand.

Similarly, the French would prove far less frustrating to other cultures if approached with the metaphor of "the French Vineyard" in mind, Mr. Gannon said. "France is a heavily agricultural country, much more so than Germany or the United States," he noted. That rural element, combined with a Cartesian educational system that emphasizes rational thought and mathematics, plants a perfectionist in the vineyard—a relationship reflected everywhere in France.

"You touch an apple in a shop in Paris and they get annoyed because you are violating the perfect picture they have developed there," Mr. Gannon said. Try to close a deal with a French business executive you met only recently? Same reaction.

15   "The French want to know you, and they really won't deal with you until they get that," he said. "In the vineyard you nurture relationships."

For Spanish society, the metaphor is the bullfight, "which really reflects Spanish culture, and is not a sport whatsoever," Mr. Gannon said. It is the proud individualism of the matador, the gang-like relationship of those in the bullring that reflects the personal relationship in Spain.

The Italian opera metaphor, he said, mirrors a society where "the drama is much more important than the individual and where emotions are so great that an individual can't hold them inside."

The American metaphor? Football, said Mr. Gannon. "Aggressiveness and individuality. In the United States, the society is individualistic and we focus on specialization. We try to learn something really well so we as an individual can do better than anyone we are competing with. Then there's huddling: What we're really good at here is getting together on a problem, working intensely and then scattering."

I. Getting the Message

A. After reading the article, choose the best answer for each item.

1. Martin Gannon was puzzled by his wife's eating habits because he was used to
   a. eating more quickly
   b. talking at meals
   c. eating different foods

2. Gannon organized a seminar of graduate students to
   a. explore the eating habits of different cultures
   b. talk to people from many countries
   c. explore ways to characterize different societies

3. Gannon's efforts resulted in
   a. a Fulbright fellowship in Germany
   b. an extended stay in Bangkok
   c. a 500-page manuscript exploring cultural metaphors

4. The Italian opera metaphor is appropriate because
   a. Italians like opera
   b. aggressiveness and individuality are stressed
   c. drama and emotion predominate in Italian society

5. In doing his study, Gannon assumed that
   a. each society had its own metaphor
   b. people from a society cannot characterize their own culture
   c. it is unfair to make generalizations about a culture

6. Gannon's goal in establishing metaphors is to
   a. show the difficulty of analyzing another society
   b. promote understanding between groups
   c. show the difference between Americans and Europeans

Check your answers with the key on page 169. If you have made mistakes, reread the article to gain a better understanding of it.

B. Scan the article. What is the metaphor for each of these countries?

Country	Metaphor
Germany	
France	
Mexico	
Italy	
Spain	
United States	
Belgium	

II. Expanding Your Vocabulary

A. Getting Meaning from Context

Use context clues to determine the meaning of each word, found in the paragraph indicated in parentheses. Choose the correct definition.

1. thoroughly (2):   a. aggressively   b. completely
2. harmonious (5):   a. without conflict   b. full of music
3. potent (6):   a. physically strong   b. effective
4. credits (8):   a. gives as the cause   b. puts trust in
5. field (8):   a. land for crops   b. area of study
6. dynamics (10):   a. forces or principles by   b. prosperity and growth
                               which a society works
7. violating (14):   a. stealing   b. disturbing, spoiling
8. nurture (15):   a. give food to   b. let grow slowly and with
                                                             care

B. Reading for Suggested Meanings

Answer these questions.

1. In the headline, *cliché* means an overused or stereotyped expression. Which word is more positive—*metaphor* or *cliché*?

2. In paragraph 14, to show the metaphor for France, Gannon gives an example of touching an apple in a shop. What does the example show about France?

3. In paragraph 18, when football players *huddle*, they get together and discuss the next play they are going to make. Why is huddling a good way to describe American society according to Gannon?

C. Working with Abstract Nouns

Abstract nouns tell about general qualities. Many are used in this article to describe cultures. Complete each definition with the correct abstract noun.

aggressiveness   efficiency   rigidity
conformity   individualism

1. _____ means the ability to produce good results without waste of time.

2. _____ means being energetic and quick to attack.

3. _____ means that a person's self-expression is as important as the group to which he or she belongs.

4. _____ means following the generally accepted rules.

5. _____ means not being able to change from a set plan of action.

III. Analyzing Paragraphs

Answer the following questions about the structure of the article.

1. Paragraphs 1 through 4 contrast the eating patterns of what two cultures? What are the differences that Gannon observes?

2. How did these observations lead to the generalization that is made in paragraph 5?

3. Paragraphs 6 and 7 give the immediate effects of Gannon's realizations about cultural mind-sets. What were they?

4. Paragraph 8 discusses the influence of other disciplines on the study of metaphors. What two areas contributed?

5. Paragraphs 9 through 18 describe the various metaphors that Gannon developed. Why does he discuss the German metaphor for four paragraphs?

6. Does this article have a conclusion? Is ending with an example a good strategy or would a more formal ending be better?

IV. Talking and Writing

Discuss the following topics. Then choose one of them to write about.

1. What might be the problems involved in characterizing a culture with metaphors?

2. Do you think that Gannon's metaphors are well chosen? Can you think of an alternate metaphor for any of the cultures he studied?

3. Develop a metaphor for your native culture if Gannon hasn't already discussed it, or provide a different metaphor from the one Gannon has chosen.

Opinion

Hold Your Nose at the Steak House

Previewing the Article

Each year more than 6.7 billion hamburgers are sold at fast food restaurants in the United States, where "beef is king." In fact, many developed nations emphasize beef in their diets, and some economies are based almost entirely on the raising of cattle. But Jeremy Rifkin, the author of the article you are about to read, has a "beef" (slang for a complaint) about beef.

Raising and consuming cattle, he argues, harms the environment and undermines human health. This article uses many statistics and makes many claims against beef. It also criticizes government policies toward beef.

Before You Read

Before you read the article, discuss these questions.
1. What are the main foods in the diet of your native country? Is beef one of them?
2. Are you or is anyone you know a vegetarian? Do you believe that this is a healthy way to live?

As You Read

As you read, try to find at least three harmful effects of cattle raising on the environment.

Hold Your Nose
at the Steak House

By Jeremy Rifkin

WASHINGTON—In the United States beef is king. More than 6.7 billion hamburgers were sold last year at fast food restaurants alone. The average American consumes the meat of seven 1,100-pound (500-kilogram) steers in a lifetime. Some 100,000 cattle are slaughtered every 24 hours.

In South America the cattle population is approaching the human population. In Australia it has exceeded it.

Beef has been central to the American experience. Entrance into the beef culture was viewed by many immigrants as a rite of passage into the middle class. Commenting on the failure of European socialism to gain a foothold in America, Werner Sombart, a German economist, wrote: "On the shoals of roast beef and apple pie, all socialist utopias founder."

Now, the good life promised by the beef culture has changed into an environmental and social nightmare for the planet.

5   Cattle raising is a primary factor in the destruction of the world's remaining tropical rain forests. Since 1960 more than a quarter of all Central American forests have been razed to make pastures for cattle. In South America, 38 percent of all the Amazon forest cleared has been for cattle ranching.

The impact of cattle extends well beyond the rain forest. According to a 1991 report prepared for the United Nations, as much as 85 percent of the rangeland in the Western United States is being destroyed by overgrazing and other problems.

Nearly half the water used each year in the United States goes to grow feed and provide drinking water for cattle and other livestock. A 1992 study by the California Department of Water Resources reported that more than 1,200 gallons (4,500 liters) of water are required to produce an 8-ounce (220-gram) boneless steak in California.

Cattle raising is even a significant factor in global warming. The burning of tropical forests to clear land for pasture releases millions of tons of carbon dioxide into the atmosphere each year. In addition, it is estimated that the earth's 1.28 billion cattle and other cud-chewing animals are responsible for 12 percent of the methane emitted into the atmosphere.

The beef addiction of the United States and other industrialized countries has also contributed to the global food crisis. Cattle and other livestock consume more than 70 percent of the grain produced in the United States and about a third of the world's total grain harvest—while nearly a billion people suffer from chronic undernutrition.

10   If the American land now used to grow livestock feed were converted to grow grain for human consumption, America could feed an additional 400 million people.

Despite the grim facts, the U.S. government continues to pursue policies that support cattle production and beef consumption. For example, at the same time that the surgeon general is warning Americans to reduce their consumption of saturated fat, the Department of Agriculture's Beef Promotion and Research Board is trying to convince Americans to eat more beef. This year the board is expected to spend $45 million on advertising.

Equally troubling is the government's grading system to measure the value of beef. Established in 1927, the system grades beef on fat content: the higher the fat "marbling," the better the beef. By favoring fat over lean beef, the Agriculture Department has helped promote greater amounts of saturated fat in the American diet and contributed to rising health care costs.

Finally, the government has been virtually subsidizing Western cattle ranchers, providing cheap access to millions of acres of public land. Today 30,000 ranchers in 11 Western states pay less than $1.92 a month per animal for the right to graze cattle on nearly 300 million acres (120 million hectares) of public land. In 1986 the Reagan administration estimated the market value for pasturing cattle on the same land to be between $6.40 and $9.50 per month.

The government giveaway program has resulted in the destruction of native habitats, wildlife and the erosion of land.

15   The government's antiquated cattle and beef policies must be overhauled. The Agriculture Department, as it tried to do with the "Eating Right" pyramid, which was abandoned under pressure from the meat industry, needs to shift its priorities from promoting beef consumption to promoting a more balanced diet with less saturated fat. The department's grading system should be restructured, with new classifications that elevate the status of leaner cuts of beef.

Congress should pass legislation to ensure that ranchers pay the market value for leased public lands. And it should reduce the public acreage available to ranchers, to help restore the Western grasslands.

The writer, an environmental activist, is author of "Beyond Beef: The Rise and Fall of the Cattle Culture." He contributed this comment to The New York Times.

I. Getting the Message

After reading the article, indicate if each item is true (*T*) or false (*F*).

_____ 1. This article is mainly about world hunger.

_____ 2. Immigrant populations in the United States viewed consumption of beef as a sign of becoming part of the middle class.

_____ 3. A third of the grain harvest is eaten by cattle and other animals raised for food.

_____ 4. One way that cattle raising contributes to the process of global warming is by the burning of rain forests that is done to clear land for ranching.

_____ 5. The U.S. government's beef grading system rewards beef that is low in fat.

_____ 6. The U.S. government's land program is designed to minimize the amount of national land being used for grazing.

_____ 7. One point the author states directly is that it would be a good idea to turn some land now used to raise cattle into land used to grow grain to feed people.

Check your answers with the key on page 169. If you have made mistakes, reread the article to gain a better understanding of it.

II. Expanding Your Vocabulary

A. Getting Meaning from Context

Use context clues to determine the meaning of each word or phrase, found in the paragraph indicated in parentheses. Choose the correct definition.

1.	slaughtered (1):	a.	used	b. killed
2.	central (3):	a.	of major importance	b. at a center location
3.	rite of passage (3):	a.	movement to a new status in society	b. movement across the ocean
4.	nightmare (4):	a.	a difficult situation	b. a dream
5.	impact (6):	a.	problem	b. effect
6.	addiction (9):	a.	compulsive need for	b. strong preference for
7.	chronic (9):	a.	continual	b. temporary
8.	pursue (11):	a.	chase and try to catch	b. follow a course of action
9.	promote (12, 15):	a.	contribute to the growth of	b. raise to a better job

B. Defining Useful Vocabulary

Match each word with its definition.

1. subsidize   _____ right to use

2. undernutrition   _____ something given with nothing received in return

3. consumption   _____ using up, eating
4. giveaway   _____ assist by giving money or financial favors
5. grim   _____ particular area where a kind of animal lives
6. access   _____ not having enough to eat
7. habitat   _____ gloomy, depressing
8. rangeland   _____ open lands where cattle are raised

C. Practicing Useful Vocabulary

Complete the sentences with words from exercise B.

1. The _____ of beef is common in the diet of some countries, while many people in poorer countries suffer from _____.

2. The U.S. government policies _____ cattle ranchers by giving them _____ to public land at a very low cost. Some people object to this government _____.

3. The picture of the effects of beef consumption that the author presents is _____.

III. Analyzing Paragraphs

Statistics can be effective in an opinion article because they give support to the ideas expressed. Paragraphs 9 through 11 develop the effects of the beef addiction on the global food crisis and American attitudes toward that crisis. Below are some statistics given in these paragraphs that relate to these effects. Complete each phrase. The first one has been done for you.

70 percent of the grain produced in the United States

a third of _____

400 million _____

$45 million _____

Find three other statistics about cattle raising that are used in the article. List them.

IV. Talking and Writing

Discuss the following topics. Then choose one of them to write about.

1. This article discusses the conflict between the custom of beef consumption and the quality of the global environment. Can you think of a solution to this problem that could accommodate both sides?

2. Do you think that people will make changes in their personal lives to solve environmental problems? Have you made any such changes?

3. Convince beef-eating people that a different diet would be healthier for them to follow. Give at least three reasons why this alternative diet would be better.

FOCUS ON THE NEWSPAPER

Opinion

Analyzing Editorials; Letters to the Editor; Political Cartoons

While news stories are *objective* and do not overtly express a viewpoint, many newspapers have special pages reserved for presenting opinions. The opinion pages contain *subjective* views. Here is what you'll usually find on them:

- *Editorial articles* that contain the views of the editorial board of the newspaper and of other journalists who write for the paper. Often a newspaper is known for having a certain political slant, for example, favoring a certain political party. This slant, or viewpoint, is usually clearly expressed in editorials. Often the editorials will explain the reasons for a point of view.

- *Political cartoons* that illustrate by means of a drawing a view on issues in the news

- *Letters to the editor*, submitted by readers stating their views, often in response to news and opinion articles that have been printed in the newspaper

Editorials

While a headline in the news section might read "New Government Bill on Education," the opinion section would contain articles that evaluate the new education bill. A headline in the opinion section might read "Revisions Needed to Make Education Policy Effective." The headline and the accompanying article present a *judgment* on the event. They take a position on the issue in the news. Taking a clear position on an issue is what distinguishes opinion articles from other articles in a newspaper.

Sometimes opinion pages present opposing views on the same news event: "Bad Planning on Education Policy" one article may read, while another may say "New Education Bill a Good First Step." This helps readers see both sides of an issue and perhaps clarify their own ideas on the topic.

Exercise 1: What's the Opinion?

Analyze an editorial or other opinion article by answering these questions.

Analyzing an Editorial/Opinion Article

1. Who wrote the article? Does it express the opinion of an individual or of the newspaper? How do you know? _____

2. What key words in the headline or first paragraph let you know the opinion expressed in the article? _____

3. What is the issue discussed in the article? _____
    _____

4. Is the scope of the issue local, national or international? _____
    _____

5. What is the opinion of the newspaper or the writer about the issue? _____
    _____

6. What are the reasons the newspaper or writer gives to support the position taken?
    _____
    _____

7. What is your opinion on the issue? _____
    _____

Letters to the Editor

Letters to the editor provide readers with a forum in which they can express their ideas on issues in the news or on the opinions expressed in the newspaper.

Exercise 2: What Are People Talking About?

Look at current issues of the newspaper for letters to the editors. List three issues that currently interest people, judging from the letters to the editor.

_____

_____

Exercise 3: Get in the News

Draft a brief letter to the editor about a subject in the news about which you have an opinion. Remember to express a clear main idea and provide reasons to support your opinion.

 ## Political Cartoons

Political cartoons illustrate some aspect of a political issue, often in simplified terms. Yet often a picture can be very effective in dramatizing an issue. One device commonly used in political cartoons is *caricature*, in which the physical features of a person in the news are exaggerated.

Exercise 4: A Picture Is Worth a Thousand Words

Find a political cartoon in a recent newspaper. Answer these questions.

Analyzing a Political Cartoon

1. Who drew the cartoon? _____

2. Who or what is pictured in the cartoon? _____
   _____

3. What is the language in the cartoon? Is there a caption on the cartoon? Are they words spoken by the characters? How do the words help you understand the cartoon? _____
   _____

4. What is the issue presented in the cartoon? _____
   _____

5. What position on the issue does the cartoonist take? _____
   _____

6. Is the cartoon humorous? satirical? Explain your answer. _____
   _____

7. Did you find the cartoon hard to understand? If so, what information about current events do you need to understand the cartoon? _____
   _____

Exercise 5: Do You Get It?

Clip a cartoon from a recent newspaper. Discuss your cartoons in small groups. Use the questions in exercise 4 to help you analyze the cartoon's meaning.

Business

Business

Sociology of the Kimono: Everything Old Is Young

Previewing the Article

There's a familiar saying in the business world: to be a success, you need only one great idea. Sueko Otsuka had her brainstorm about 40 years ago, when she cut the kimono into a two-piece outfit. That was the beginning that led many designers after her to modify the kimono in order to keep it marketable. The new kimono is inexpensive, easy to wear and easy to care for.

If there is a moral to this story, it is this: traditions are more likely to survive if they can adapt to changing times. Does that mean that the traditional, authentic kimono is only a memory? No, it's still around, too.

Before You Read

Before you read the article, discuss these questions.
1. Are there traditional articles of clothing still widely worn in your country? Have they been modernized in some way?
2. Can you think of other items from past centuries that have been adapted to modern times?

As You Read

As you read, look for information about how the new kimono differs from the traditional one.

Sociology of the Kimono: Everything Old Is Young

By Kay Itoi

TOKYO—When Sueko Otsuka cut her kimono at its waist nearly 40 years ago, efforts to preserve Japan's native dress as a contemporary garment began. Her two-piece kimono could be put on as easily as Western-style clothing: It took only 30 seconds to get into it, compared with 20 minutes or more for the traditional kimono.

At 87, Otsuka still runs a sewing school in central Tokyo, and her famous garment is still on sale at large emporiums such as Takashimaya. And if she is no longer startling Japanese consumers and fashion experts with similar innovations, she can be credited with launching a national preoccupation with the kimono's place in the modern world.

In its straight, simple lines and austere, geometric shape, the garment is universally accepted as an important influence in the work of such fashion figures as Issey Miyake and Yohji Yamamoto (whose film, "Notes on Clothes and Cities," made with Wim Wenders, has just opened in Paris and Tokyo). In ways not always apparent to the Western eye, these designers are carrying the kimono worldwide.

But younger Tokyo designers are working even more directly with the garment itself. They are preserving its line and rich colors while radically re-cutting it and using variations of its wide *obi* belt to eliminate zippers, buttons and other staples of modern dress.

5   "Everything we wear has been an imitation of Western clothing," says Eiji Miyamoto, a weaver of traditional Japanese cloth and a designer of kimono-inspired contemporary clothing. "When you want to create something unique, you cannot help but go back to the kimono."

The traditional kimono is one of the few things Japan left out of the modernization process it abruptly began late in the last century. It is seldom worn now except on special occasions

such as weddings, funerals and tea ceremonies because it simply does not fit the pace of life in today's Japan, and it is also too expensive—costing on an average between 300,000 to 500,000 yen (about $2,130 to $3,500).

Oddly, schools teaching how to dress in the traditional kimono are booming, and manufacturers are struggling to keep the garment alive: "You can present your 'Japaneseness' most directly when you are in a ki-

© Mark E. Gibson

The kimono, although it may be "modernized," is still worn in Japan for special occasions—and sometimes even as a fashion statement.

mono," said Tamako Sonoda, director of the Shizu Naganuma Kimono School, a nationwide chain. "Because we are in this internationalized society, I believe all the more that the kimono will never disappear."

But it is an endangered species nonetheless. And the keys to its survival now are its uniqueness and the imaginations of designers and retailers.

"Being fashionable is being different from others," said Hiroko Wada, who launched her own line of kimonos in 1977 and sells them under the brand name of Bushoan. "Young girls don't care about the kimono's cultural importance; they wear it to be distinctive."

10   If the Otsuka two-piece was an experiment, Wada's kimono was Japan's first "new kimono," a generic term quickly coined in fashion circles. To begin with, it was all ready-to-wear—a major innovation in a world strictly geared to made-to-order garments.

She designed not only the kimono itself, but also all the undergarments, the obi belt, white *tabi* (socks) and *zori* (sandals). Each of these items was produced and sold by specialized designers and retailers.

The central idea was to lower the cost to something under 150,000 yen. Wada replaced traditional silk with polyester to make it washable. In addition, the new kimono was sold at department stores and shopping malls instead of traditional *gofukuya,* or dry-goods stores.

She also ignored the rules of colors. In the past, age, marital status, season and occasion all went into determining the color, pattern and shape of the kimono a woman would select. Accordingly, younger women were to wear vivid colors; but because these tend toward the "too cute," Wada bowed to modern fashion and used rather sober, calm colors such as gray, dark green and maroon.

When it appeared in many fashionable magazines and on television shows, the new kimono caused a sensation among retailers and manufacturers. More than 60 similar brands came out in the early 1980s, but few of these have survived the end of that particular boom.

15   The kimono's life in the late 20th century did not have to be so difficult, many in the industry believe. When the war ended and Japan's values were being shaped anew, it was a perfect moment to rethink the kimono along with almost everything else that remained of the old order. Eating, sleeping, dressing—all such aspects of Japanese life changed. But the kimono industry stayed the same, never breaking formality.

"The problem is that the industry did not keep up with changing consumers," said Kunio Ono, marketing manager at Ichida & Co., the nation's largest manufacturer and wholesaler of kimonos. In the past several years alone, Ichida's annual sales have shrunk from more than half of the company's total to 36 percent.

Ono observed that the market is now split in two: There is one for conventional and expensive kimonos and another for new ones. Several years ago, Ichida launched Yume Kobo, a new brand in the latter category; he claims it already earns 2 billion yen annually.

Ichida executives see the preservation of the traditional kimono as a company mission of sorts. Among other things, it sponsors young artists specialized in the traditional handwork of kimono production. At the same time, the industry is trying to encourage more women to wear new kimonos for less formal occasions that follow formal receptions in Japan.

"The traditional segment of the business will not dramatically expand," Ono acknowledged. "The industry's existence depends on the other part now—on the new kimono."

I. Getting the Message

A. After reading the article, choose the best answer for each item.

1. In the Japanese kimono industry, Sueko Otsuka is important because
   a. she is designing the newest kimonos
   b. she is teaching the young designers how to sew
   c. she started the trend of modernizing the kimono

2. The traditional kimono has become less popular in Japan because
   a. modern Japanese women don't like dark colors
   b. it is expensive and time-consuming to put on
   c. it is no longer manufactured in Japan

3. Modern Japanese women often wear kimonos
   a. to weddings and funerals
   b. to work or school
   c. as a robe around the house

4. According to Wada, many younger Japanese women wear kimonos
   a. to return to the past
   b. to be different
   c. because kimonos are lightweight

5. The Ichida Company, which makes traditional kimonos, is described as
   a. about to go out of business
   b. expecting to sell many more traditional kimonos
   c. trying to preserve the traditional kimono

Check your answers with the key on page 169. If you have made mistakes, reread the article to gain a better understanding of it.

B. Decide if each of the following descriptions relates to the traditional, to the new kimono or to both traditional and new. Write *T* for traditional, *N* for new or *B* for both.

_____ 1. two-piece   _____ 5. sold in department stores

_____ 2. worn with sandals   _____ 6. made to order

_____ 3. made of silk   _____ 7. washable

_____ 4. made of polyester   _____ 8. can be in dark colors

II. Expanding Your Vocabulary

Getting Meaning from Context

Use context clues to determine the meaning of each word, found in the paragraph indicated in parentheses. Choose the correct definition.

1. emporiums (2):   a. places to shop   b. empires
2. preoccupation (2):   a. a former job   b. the taking over of some-one's thoughts
3. apparent (3):   a. able to be seen   b. clothing
4. keys (8):   a. means or ways   b. utensils for opening locks
5. coined (10):   a. invented a phrase   b. made a coin
6. circles (10):   a. round shapes   b. groups of people
7. wholesaler (16):   a. a company that sells large quantities of merchandise to retail businesses   b. a company that sells directly to individual consumers of the product
8. the latter (17):   a. the last of two things mentioned   b. the first of two things mentioned
9. mission (18):   a. a group of people sent to do a task   b. a specific task for a group to achieve

---

III. Working with Idioms

Study the meanings of these idioms and expressions.

the Western eye (3) = the viewpoint of people from the Western Hemisphere

booming (7) = increasing or expanding rapidly

ready-to-wear (10) = made to sell to the general public

made-to-order (10) = custom-made for one specific buyer

the old order (15) = past traditions or way of life

keep up with (16) = go at the same speed, stay up to date

Answer these questions.

1. According to paragraph 3, what is not always apparent to the *Western eye*?

2. In paragraph 7, schools to teach women how to put on the traditional kimono are *booming*. Why is that odd?

3. According to paragraph 15, after World War II, did much remain of the *old order* in Japan?

4. Is the new kimono *made-to-order* or *ready-to-wear*?

IV. Making Sense of Sentences

The first sentence in paragraph 11 uses a pattern with *not only* and *but also* to add together two ideas. This pattern often suggests that the second trait (following *but also*) is more unusual or unexpected than the first.

Example: The traditional kimono is *not only* expensive *but also* difficult to put on.

Use this pattern to complete these sentences. Reread the paragraphs for help, if necessary.

1. Sueko Otsuka not only _____ but also _____. (2)

2. The new kimono is not only _____ but also _____. (12)

3. Today kimonos are sold not only _____ but also _____. (12)

V. Talking and Writing

Discuss the following topics. Then choose one of them to write about.

1. Why does it take 20 minutes to put on the traditional kimono? Do research to find the answer. (You may be able to interview someone who knows about kimonos.)

2. Is there a disappearing tradition in your native country that some people are fighting to maintain? What is it? Do you believe it's important to continue it? Why, or why not?

3. Do you think the clothing that men and women wear today is comfortable, practical and attractive? What do you like, and what do you dislike? If you were a clothing designer, what changes would you make in fashions?

Business

For Eskimo Artists Seeking Inspiration, Money Talks

Previewing the Article

When is primitive art no longer primitive? Does change in traditional forms always mean a change for the worse? For example, does it mean that art no longer expresses the native culture? The following article discusses these and other important questions about artistic expression. It also discusses the relationship between the artist and the purchaser of art. Is artistic expression negatively affected when art is altered to increase sales?

Before You Read

Before you read the article, discuss these questions.
1. How do primitive cultures differ from those considered civilized?
2. What are some characteristics of primitive art? Why do you think it is very popular today?
3. What people, animals and activities are the usual subjects of Eskimo art? Look at some photographs of Eskimo art to determine this.

As You Read

As you read, look for answers to these questions.
1. How has Eskimo art changed in recent years?
2. Does the author express his opinion about whether the changes in Eskimo art are good or bad?

For Eskimo Artists Seeking Inspiration, Money Talks

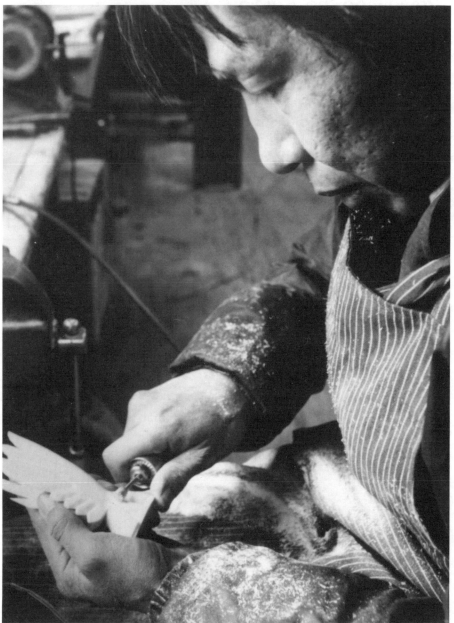

© Mark E. Gibson

Eskimo artist carving a traditional animal sculpture—such artists now can be in close contact with art markets in large cities.

By William Claiborne
Washington Post Service

HOLMAN, Northwest Territories—According to animistic beliefs held for thousands of years by Eskimo stone carvers in the Arctic tundra of Canada's far north, the soul of a piece of stone whispers to the artist before the first strike of the chisel and guides his creativity until the work is finished.

But more likely in modern-day Arctic communities such as this isolated island hamlet in the Beaufort Sea, the voice speaking to the artist comes from the other end of a display terminal of a video-telephone linkup. And it is not the soul of the stone that is heard but that of a big-city art dealer with a profitable deal in mind.

High technology and sophisticated marketing techniques are helping to drive the Arctic's $48 million arts-and-crafts industry, propelling some formerly impoverished aboriginals into comfortable lifestyles and generating wider interest in sculptures and primitive prints by Eskimos, who in this region of the western Arctic are known as Inuvialit and in the eastern Arctic are called Inuit.

Some purists see such advances as a cultural intrusion into an ancient and remote civilization that could dilute and ultimately spoil a unique art form.
5 "I'm not so sure it's a good thing at all," said John Bailey, chairman of the Northwest Territories' Wildlife Management Advisory Council. "Whose expression is coming out in the end—the artist's or the dealer's?"

Gordon Peters, manager of the government-assisted Holman Eskimo Cooperative, defends the use of high-powered marketing strategies as a boon to artists who for years were commercially exploited by white dealers before they banded together in the 1960s to command hefty prices for their work.

Soapstone carvings that may take three or four days' work now can bring an artist $2,000 or more, and the 1,200 limited-edition prints being produced this year by this community's 20 artists are bringing in an average price of $350.

Pointing to the video monitor he has been using for three years to help market Eskimo art throughout Canada and abroad, Mr. Peters, 33, said: "It takes away the guesswork. A dealer can have an idea of what a carving is really worth, and he's more likely to buy it."

Mr. Peters, who lives in this Eskimo settlement on Victoria Island, about 300 miles (500 kilometers) northeast of the district capital of Inuvik on the Arctic mainland, establishes telephone-video links with dealers in Toronto, Montreal and other cities. Placing a carving in front of a small camera, he transmits front, back and side views to potential buyers.

10 Similar video screening methods are used by the Hudson's Bay Co. outlet in Holman and by other agents for Eskimo artists throughout the Arctic.

Mr. Peters says that sometimes, particularly in the case of commissioned work, a buyer will ask that changes be made in uncompleted carvings—a practice that purists complain is alien to native artisans and corrupting of their craft.

"This leads to better understanding between the artist and buyer," Mr. Peters said. "One time I paid a carver $1,200 for a carving. But I only got $200 for it, because when I sent it down there they thought it was too gruesome. The television could have avoided that."

Last year, native arts and crafts were the basis of an $80 million wholesale business across Canada, of which Inuit carvings and prints made up a substantial share and provided financial independence for about 5,500 of the Northwest Territories' 18,360 Eskimos.

For more than 300 years, Inuit carvings were brought south by Jesuit missionaries, the white crews of whaling ships and traders working for the Hudson's Bay Co. But it was not until the 1940s that a commercial market began to develop in Montreal and, gradually, in cities around the world.

15 Consumer demand is gradually altering the style of Inuit art in ways that go beyond the use of video screening by dealers.

Traditionally, Eskimos used soapstone for their printing blocks, which in recent years were destroyed after limited editions of no more than 50 prints were produced. However, they stopped using that technique in 1985 and turned to woodblock printing and relatively modern lithography techniques.

Increasingly, buyer demand led the artists to branch out into stencil art, using sheets of plastic and brushed paint, and into free-form work using crayon and felt-tip pen. As the demand for color has increased, more and more Eskimo artists are abandoning traditional one-dimensional, black-and-white prints and are expanding into impressionist and modern art to suit the tastes of their clients.

"There's less demand now for the old-style black block prints," Mr. Peters said. "People want more color, and the artists are responding to the market."

▃▃▃ I. Getting the Message

A. After reading the article, indicate if each statement is true (*T*) or false (*F*).

_____ 1. TV sets attached to telephone lines let art dealers see Eskimo works in progress.

_____ 2. Contemporary Eskimo artists use exactly the same materials that their ancestors did.

_____ 3. Today, art dealers make a lot of money on Eskimo art, but the Eskimo artists make very little.

_____ 4. The people whom the author calls purists want Eskimo art to be unaffected by the modern world.

_____ 5. Some buyers request that the Eskimo artists make changes in a carving.

_____ 6. The author of this article says that, in his opinion, Eskimo art is being spoiled by high technology and modern marketing techniques.

Check your answers with the key on page 169. If you have made mistakes, reread the article to gain a better understanding of it.

B. Decide if each of the following descriptions relates to traditional Eskimo art or new Eskimo art. Write *T* for traditional or *N* for new.

_____ 1. soapstone blocks   _____ 4. maximum of 50 prints

_____ 2. crayon or pen   from each block

_____ 3. many colors   _____ 5. wood blocks

II. Expanding Your Vocabulary

Getting Meaning from Context

Use context clues to determine the meaning of each word or phrase, found in the paragraph indicated in parentheses. Then choose the correct definition of each.

1. drive (3):
   a. carry in a vehicle
   b. cause to have force and energy

2. intrusion (4):
   a. unwanted influence
   b. unexpected visit

3. dilute (4):
   a. cause to use a mix of materials
   b. make less powerful and genuine

4. boon (6):
   a. a benefit
   b. a very loud noise

5. hefty (6)
   a. heavy in weight
   b. high in cost

6. limited-edition (7):
   a. as many copies as people want to buy
   b. a relatively small number of copies

7. average (7):
   a. usual, expected
   b. the arithmetical middle

8. abandoning (17):
   a. leaving
   b. no longer using

III. Working with Idioms

Study the meanings of these idioms and expressions.

money talks (from the headline) = possibility of profit influences behavior

high as in **high technology** (3) and **high-powered** (6) = more than usual, advanced or sophisticated

band together (6) = unite, form a group, organize

bring in (7) = produce, earn as income

take away (8) = remove

guesswork (8) = uncertainty, need to guess

branch out (17) = try something new (usually in a business)

Answer these questions.

1. How does a video monitor take away *guesswork* from the marketing of Eskimo art?
2. Why are Eskimo artists *branching out*?
3. According to paragraph 6, who *banded together* to avoid being exploited?
4. Has *high technology* helped or harmed the Eskimos of Canada?
5. Does this article prove or disprove the popular saying *money talks*?

IV. Analyzing Paragraphs

In well-written articles, each paragraph or set of paragraphs performs a specific purpose. Reread the paragraphs indicated, looking for their function and type of development. Then answer the questions.

1. In paragraphs 1 and 2, which of the following is the author doing: explaining cause and effect, contrasting the past and present, or defining artistic terms?

2. In paragraphs 3 and 4, what two reasons are given for recent changes in Eskimo art?

3. Paragraphs 4 and 5 present ideas that contrast with ideas presented earlier in the article. These paragraphs quote people who don't like the recent changes in Eskimo art. What is their objection to the changes?

4. In paragraphs 7 and 13, the author explains how these changes have affected the lives of some Eskimos. What has been the major effect?

5. Paragraphs 16 through 18 give examples of new developments in Eskimo art. List three examples of these.

V. Talking and Writing

Discuss the following topics. Then choose one of them to write about.

1. How has high technology changed the marketing of Eskimo art? Reread the article carefully, and then summarize the information you find.

2. How does the primitive art of your native country compare to Eskimo art? Point out similarities and differences.

3. Some people feel that technology has spoiled many things. Can you think of something (for example, a product, job or form of recreation) that you liked better the old-fashioned way?

Business

*Anxiously, Some Everyday Russians Are Making Their Own
Mark on the Economy*

Previewing the Article

When you read about the Zverevs and the Stepanovs, you will get a sense
of how many Russians are living these days. During this transitional period,
when Russia is switching from a government-owned and government-
operated economy to a free market economy, life is difficult for almost
everyone. People must develop new job skills and new attitudes toward
work. They must live with uncertainties they never experienced before.

The extended family described in this article is a microcosm of the
common Russian experience today. These people are adapting to great
change with courage, initiative, ingenuity and optimism.

Before You Read

Before you read the article, discuss these questions.
1. What are the main differences between a communistic and a
    capitalistic economy?

2. What current economic changes are taking place in the former So-
    viet Union and other countries that were part of the Eastern bloc?
    What do you know from news reports and from your reading?

As You Read

As you read, look for examples of changes in the attitudes of the family
members toward their jobs, their future and each other.

Anxiously, Some Everyday Russians Are Making Their Own Mark on the Economy

By Steven Erlanger
New York Times Service

MOSCOW—The Zverev family is getting by in the new Russia, thank you, although it's not easy. They are grumpy about a confused present and nervous about the future, about whether Russia's bet on the West, on democracy and a market economy is going to pay off.

But they are finding ways to make more money and to make their lives more rewarding as well. That they have coped with the radical changes in economic life—rampant inflation's far higher prices, but also more possibilities for even the modestly clever—testifies to the survival of initiative and entrepreneurship under Soviet communism.

In a sense, the most fundamental changes are hidden, bubbling up through the thick sludge of Soviet habits and conceptions. Attitudes in government ministries may not be changing much, but people like the Zverevs are learning that they can and must take responsibility for their own lives.

The family—a couple on pension and their two married daughters, their husbands and children—was approached as they washed a battered brown Zhiguli in the courtyard of a Moscow apartment building.

5 "For 70 years, people got paid the same no matter how well they worked," said Natasha S. Stepanov, a 25-year-old mother of two. "Now we live day by day, with everything changing, so you never know what anything will cost. Some want to go back, because it was easier."

Her sister, Nina S. Zverev, 28, is married to one of Russia's new businessmen. "But we can also see a little into the future," she said, "where people with good qualifications and hard work can find their place."

Mrs. Stepanov shook her head. Her husband is a butcher, but it is she, with a newly found talent for dressmaking and design, who keeps the family solvent. "There are a lot of ordinary workers who want to return to the way it was," she said. "But I think it's much better to live through this change and suffer now. To go backward again would be horrible, absolutely horrible."

Mikhail I. Stepanov and his wife are a striking example of the intermingling of Russian life's old patterns and new.

Mr. Stepanov, also 25, has what at first seems to be a typical worker's existence under the old regime—regular hours at an institute cafeteria, access to certain bargains and small privileges, a taste for vodka and television, and a hectic life in a small, three-room apartment in which his in-laws and his wife and their two young children all live.

10 But the substructure of his life has changed fundamentally, in ways he does not always understand.

The cafeteria in which he works, at the Institute of Thermal Technology, which does research on heating equipment, used to be Cafeteria No. 20 of the Kirovsky District.

Now it is Cafeteria No. 20—Avangard, a fancy name for the newly privatized business that issued shares to its workers last September and still offers a decent lunch for the equivalent of about 20 cents, which Mr. Stepanov regards as expensive.

Their trade union has ceased to operate, but most institute employees still get lunch vouchers worth 10 or 15 rubles.

Mr. Stepanov, an army veteran who served in Siberia as a cook, is running a bit to fat. His mother worked at an engine factory; his father worked at the thermal institute, as does an older brother. The couple met at the brother's wedding, and Mr. Stepanov knows he was lucky. His wife is energetic and shrewd, and he seems happy when she tells him what to do.

15 She pushed him to buy 8,000 rubles' worth of shares in the cafeteria, all they felt they could afford. The ruble is currently trading at about 130 to the dollar.

For Mr. Stepanov, the monthly dividend of about 500 rubles is more than half his official salary of 850 rubles a month after taxes. Some friends who bought more shares are making as much as 2,000 rubles a month in dividends.

> 'For 70 years, people got paid the same no matter how well they worked. Now we live day by day, with everything changing, so you never know what anything will cost. Some want to go back, because it was easier.'
>
> **A 25-year-old mother of two.**

In Russia, the average monthly salary is 2,500 to 3,500 rubles, depending on whom you believe. But as a butcher in a cafeteria, Mr. Stepanov has access to food at cheap prices, and he brings a lot home.

In the Soviet Communist tradition, such workers would simply steal food, on the accepted notion that "everything belongs to everyone, or no one, so it might as well belong to me." But Mr. Stepanov insists that in the privatized Cafe Avangard there is a clear relationship between profits and dividends, so there is little stealing.

But he can still buy a kilogram (2.2 pounds) of veal for 30 rubles, less than half the price in stores—when it can be found—and 10 eggs for 15 rubles, instead of 21 rubles in stores. And access to cheap food means access to favors, since a kilo of veal may still buy a service, like an appointment with a good doctor on short notice or a spare part in short supply. Money is beginning to have meaning again in Russia, but in a period of shortages cheap veal can mean more than cash.

20 But besides salary, there are subsidies for children. The Stepanovs get about 160 rubles a month as a food subsidy for each of their two children, plus a yearly clothing subsidy that was 500 rubles last year may double this year. There are also 370 rubles a month for each child, which goes to the kindergarten where they spend weekdays from 8 A.M. to 5:30 P.M., leaving Mrs. Stepanov free for shopping and getting her work done.

Previously, Mr. Stepanov said, they could not get by unless they lived with Mrs. Stepanov's parents. Now with huge price increases since January, "even that wouldn't be enough." But forced by circumstances, and suddenly finding a talent within herself,

Mrs. Stepanov began to make clothes for friends.

As a wedding present, her father-in-law gave her a German sewing machine that he got at a discount through the institute, which had done some barter trade with Germany.

She began to buy the Russian edition of the German magazine Burda, which contains patterns, and began to sew. She described how, as prices were liberalized in January, "the boyfriend of a friend of a friend" asked her to sew him a leather jacket for 2,000 rubles.

"It came out all right," she said, "and then it was one thing after another—some dresses, a man's suit. Then I wanted a coat, so I bought material enough for two, spending 2,000 rubles, and sold one for 6,000 rubles, and then bought more material."

25 In the last three months, she said proudly as she pulled out examples of her own designs, she has made a profit of 26,000 rubles, more than six times her husband's take-home pay.

Is Mr. Stepanov proud of her? "Of course," he said. "Without the sewing, we couldn't survive."

But earlier, Mrs. Stepanov said his

"male pride" had been wounded. "That I make so much money affects my husband badly," she said. "He was really angry when he realized the amount."

Even for her, she said, the current state of near hyperinflation, with prices going up 20 percent a month, creates enormous tensions.

"Almost everything I earn I spend, because I'm afraid to keep money at a time like this," Mrs. Stepanov said. "So I buy what I think I'll need for the new apartment, and I try to pay off old debts."

30 In September, they expect to move into an apartment of their own in a new cooperative.

The apartment has two rooms, plus a fair-sized kitchen and the standard prefabricated bath and toilet rooms. Although it is small and farther from the city center than her parents' place, Mrs. Stepanov is pleased because the air is cleaner.

Mr. Stepanov, who finally admitted that he hates his job but knows no other, said the apartment "is the biggest happiness we have in front of us."

I. Getting the Message

A. After reading the article, indicate if each item is true (*T*) or false (*F*). The statements are about the Russian economy.

_____ 1. Prices are going up rapidly.

_____ 2. The government owns and controls all businesses.

_____ 3. It's illegal to start your own business.

_____ 4. Retired people no longer get pensions.

_____ 5. The currency is still called the ruble.

_____ 6. The government subsidizes day care for children.

_____ 7. Families are crowded together in small apartments.

_____ 8. There are often food shortages.

Check your answers with the key on page 169. If you have made mistakes, reread the article to gain a better understanding of it.

B. Match these family members with their sources of income.

1. Nina and Natasha's parents   _____ pensions

2. Mikhail Stepanov   _____ salary and dividends

3. Natasha Stepanov   _____ profits from business

II. Expanding Your Vocabulary

A. Getting Meaning from Context

Use context clues to determine the meaning of each word, found in the
paragraph(s) indicated in parentheses. Choose the correct definition. Note
that all the words are about business.

1. inflation (2):
   a. prices rise and the value of money declines
   b. prices fall and the value of money rises

2. solvent (7):
   a. capable of paying all one's bills
   b. able to solve problems

3. shares (12, 15, 16):
   a. partial ownership of a business
   b. equal portions of a product

4. dividend (16):
   a. a bonus, something extra
   b. earnings from shares of stock

5. shortages (19):
   a. a short wait for all products
   b. not enough of some products on the market

6. discount (22):
   a. a lower price than usual
   b. giving away of a product without charge

7. profit (25):
   a. total amount of money earned
   b. money left after a business has paid all its expenses

8. debts (29):
   a. money owed
   b. money earned

B. Reading for Suggested Meanings

Answer these questions.

1. Does the *thank you* in paragraph 1 suggest that the Zverev family wants people to feel sorry for them?
2. Reread paragraphs 2 and 3.
   a. Do you think the author admires the Zverev family?
   b. What words reveal his attitude?
3. In paragraph 12, the author mentions lunch for about 20 cents *which Mr. Stepanov regards as expensive*. Does the author consider it expensive?
4. Paragraph 29 suggests that in *inflationary* times it's better to buy what you need rather than put your money in the bank. Why is that true?

III. Working with Idioms

Study the meanings of these idioms and expressions.

Phrasal verbs:
get by (1) = manage to live at a minimum level
pay off (1, 29) = be worthwhile or profitable (1); pay all that is owed (29)
go back (5) = return to an old way of doing things
come out (24) = end up, turn out

Other expressions:

making their own mark (headline) = accomplishing something that's noticed

market economy (1) = a free market, where production and prices are not controlled by the government

make money (2) = earn money

live day by day (5) = live worrying about one day at a time, without planning for the future

run a bit to fat (14) = get fat

push someone to do something (15) = urge, strongly encourage

make a profit (25) = have money left after expenses are paid

take-home pay (25) = net income, earnings received after deductions for taxes, etc.

his male pride was wounded (27) = he felt belittled or inferior because of his wife's greater success

Answer these questions.

1. How is Natasha's talent for dressmaking and design *paying off* for her?

2. Did Natasha have to *be pushed* to start her business?

3. In your opinion, which is better—to have a huge income or to just *get by*?

4. What is the biggest problem that the *market economy* has created for this family?

5. Why doesn't Natasha Stepanov want to *go back* to "the way it was"?

IV. Focusing on Style and Tone

A. *Finding the Interview in the Article*

The author of this article got his information about this family by interviewing them. But, in writing the article, he didn't use a question/answer format. Instead, he summarized some of their responses and quoted others. Imagine that you are Steven Erlanger, interviewing this Russian family. What questions would you ask to get the same information? Reread the paragraphs listed, and then write an appropriate question for each.

Example: Paragraph 26: Did your success in business bother your husband at all?

1. Paragraph 17: _____

2. Paragraph 21: _____

3. Paragraphs 21–22: _____

4. Paragraph 30: _____

B. *Showing instead of Telling*

Notice that the author doesn't tell his readers what to think about this Russian family. He presents their words and actions and lets his readers decide for themselves. What did you learn about the Zverevs and the Stepanovs from these incidents?

1. washing the car (4) _____

2. bartering with veal (19) _____

3. purchasing the sewing machine (22) _____

V. Talking and Writing

Discuss the following topics. Then choose one of them to write about.

1. Speaking from your own experience, what are some of the economic problems associated with communism and with capitalism? Which system do you think works better? Why?

2. When times are bad, families often combine their resources in order to get by. In your native country, do extended families share living quarters and resources as this Russian family does? If so, what are some of the advantages and disadvantages?

Business

King of the Court: High-Tech, High-Price Sneakers

Previewing the Article

What's in a name? About $1.7 billion if the name is Nike, Reebok, Converse, L.A. Gear and Adidas, makers of the most popular basketball shoes in the world today. With players including Chicago Bulls' superstar Michael Jordan advertising these stylish sneakers, it is anticipated that the market will continue to grow.

In the article you are about to read, the most popular brands are contrasted with each other and with the more traditional basketball shoes of the past. Also compared are the marketing techniques of the various makers of the shoes. How to sell is an essential part of any business, and some new companies have used advertising techniques as high-tech as the shoes they make.

Before You Read

Before you read the article, discuss these questions.
1. Do you own or would you like to own a pair of name-brand basketball shoes? Why, or why not?
2. Why do you think that designer labels in clothing and shoes have become so popular?

As You Read

As you read, find the main reasons why basketball shoe buyers say they are attracted to the shoes. Do you think these are good reasons?

King of the Court: High-Tech, High-Price Sneakers

By Glenn Rifkin
New York Times Service

NEW YORK—When Michael Jordan of the Chicago Bulls began advertising basketball shoes a few years ago—the Air Jordan line by Nike Inc.—he was selling high-tech style as much as performance.

Unlike their low-tech, black-and-white predecessors, today's basketball shoes are made of lightweight leathers and synthetics dyed in a dazzling array of colors with vivid, high-contrast, graphic designs. They are also constructed with sophisticated cushioning devices and fitting systems.

And they are expensive. PF Flyers and U.S. Keds, the standbys of a generation or two ago, rarely cost more than $10 or $15 a pair—roughly $20 now. Today's popular styles can cost as much as $160.

High style—and higher prices—have made basketball shoes big business. They are now the largest niche in the $7.66 billion wholesale market for sport shoes. According to the Sporting Goods Manufacturers Association, an industry group in North Palm Beach, Florida, wholesale sales of basketball shoes—high tech as well as canvas—totaled about $1.7 billion in 1990. Most of those sales—about 75 percent—were for just five brands: Nike, Reebok, Converse, L.A. Gear and Adidas.

5   The market for basketball shoes has been growing rapidly, too. Between 1986 and 1990, the market grew at a rate of about 19 percent a year, according to Sporting Goods Intelligence, an industry newsletter in Glenn Mill, Pennsylvania. Last year, largely because of the recession and market saturation, the market expanded by just 4.1 percent.

But industry analysts are hopeful that 1992 will show strong growth.

"With excitement building around the Olympics, I expect 1992 to be a peak year for basketball shoes," said

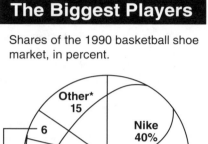

The Biggest Players

Shares of the 1990 basketball shoe market, in percent.

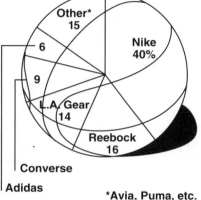

Other* 15
6
9
Nike 40%
L.A. Gear 14
Reebock 16
Converse
Adidas
*Avia, Puma, etc.

Source: *Sporting Goods Intelligence Newsletter*

Dick Silverman, associate publisher of Footwear News, a trade newspaper in New York.

When it comes to breeding, Converse Inc., the North Reading, Massachusetts, athletic-shoe maker, is the original. Converse has been making its popular All Star canvas basketball sneaker since 1917. In 1923, it renamed the shoe the Chuck Taylor All Star after Chuck Taylor, a popular basketball player of the time who joined the company as a spokesman in 1921. Converse has sold more than 500 million pairs of All Stars.

But despite Converse's early start, the market is now dominated by Nike, of Beaverton, Oregon, and Reebok, of Stoughton, Massachusetts. Nike, which sells about $500 million worth of basketball shoes a year, has about 40 percent of the market. Reebok has about 16 percent of the market. Converse retains 9 percent of the market. 10 Nike and Reebok spent about $130 million each in 1991 on television advertising for their products, in what was called the "sneaker wars."

'The shoes are genuinely better. It's not just marketing hype. No NBA player would want to go through a season with Chuck Taylor All Stars today.'
John Horan, industry analyst

The commercials featured players from the National Basketball Association and claimed the companies' high-tech shoes gave the players an edge.

"I can't deny that a lot of this is about marketing," said Peter Ruppe, Nike's manager for basketball marketing. "But the key thing is to make a great product."

While the companies' advertising appeals may be pitched to athletes, 80 percent of the sporting shoes purchased are never used in play.

"A large majority of these shoes are being worn as street wear," Silverman said. "The companies don't want to own up to that."

Even so, play-related advertising sells shoes. According to John Horan, publisher of Sporting Goods Intelligence, which surveys retailers, in 1990, 37 percent of all basketball shoe buyers based their decisions on advertising; 25 percent based their decisions on technology and 23 percent were motivated by fashion. Only 10 percent bought basketball shoes on the basis of quality and price.

15   Even its competitors admit that when it comes to marketing and promotion, Nike is without peer. Mickey Bell, executive vice president of Converse, credits Nike with changing the rules of the game in the early 1980s by focusing on marketing rather than manufacturing issues.

The breakthrough came when Nike signed rising superstar Michael Jordan and introduced the Air Jordan line in 1985.

"That changed everything," Bell said. Building brand recognition by tying it to a single star athlete fueled Nike's success.

Along with Jordan, Nike features National Basketball Association stars like David Robinson, Charles Barkley and Scottie Pippen to sell its Air Force and Air Flight lines.

Ruppe, Nike's marketing manager for basketball, acknowledges that Jordan, who is paid $6 million annually by Nike, was the "paradigm" for today's advertising.

20 Television ads featuring Jordan and film maker Spike Lee continue to win awards and drive Nike sales. Nike's overall slogan is "Just Do It." But after a stirring play in a pickup game, the cry usually heard in the commercial is: "It's gotta be the shoes!"

Ruppe said that Air Jordans, which sell for about $130, make up about 10 percent of its basketball shoe sales.

For the fall of 1992, Nike will offer 17 models of basketball shoes, ranging in price from $50 to $130.

The most popular model sells for about $75.

Reebok, which entered the basketball shoe arena in 1986, has challenged Nike with its own high-visibility marketing campaign. Its slogan is "Life is Short, Play Hard." Rather than tie its brands to a specific athlete, Reebok tries to "talk the talk and walk the walk" of the average basketball player, according to John Morgan, vice president of the performance division.

Most recently, Reebok tied its fortunes to its Pump technology, along with a new line of outdoor sneakers called Blacktop. The hugely successful Pump shoe, which incorporates an inflatable bladder into the upper portion of the sneaker, helped Reebok gain market share at Nike's expense.

25 The company has sold more than 6 million pairs of Pumps, bringing in more than $750 million in revenue since they were introduced in 1989. Reebok offers nearly a dozen models

of basketball shoes ranging in price from $50 to $160. Morgan said the company's mainstay is its $55 shoe which accounts for 40 percent of its basketball shoe sales.

"Fit is the battleground," said Nike's Ruppe. Nike continues to tinker with its Air technology, which uses lightweight stretch material along with its patented midsole system, to provide better cushioning.

Nike is intent on reducing the weight of its shoes and improving the cushioning without adding features like bladders. The hope, Ruppe said, is to offer a high-performance shoe for a lower price "to make it accessible for kids who can't spend over $100." A long list of new technologies is being incorporated into basketball shoes.

"The shoes are genuinely better," Horan said. "It's not just marketing hype. No NBA player would want to go through a season with Chuck Taylor All Stars today."

I. Getting the Message

A. After reading the article, choose the best answer for each item.

1. Unlike older basketball shoes, today's basketball shoes are
   a. made of lightweight leathers and synthetics
   b. worn only for basketball
   c. black-and-white canvas

2. Since Converse began making basketball shoes in 1917, it has
   a. constantly dominated the market
   b. moved away from North Reading, Massachusetts
   c. sold 500 million pairs of its All Stars

3. In one survey, 10 percent of high-style basketball shoe buyers based their decision on
   a. fashion
   b. quality and price
   c. technology

4. Nike is known for its strength in
   a. quality and price
   b. technology
   c. marketing and promotion

5. Rather than use specific basketball superstars, Reebok markets its Pump technology with
   a. slogans appealing to the average player
   b. movie stars' endorsements
   c. designers' endorsements

Check your answers with the key on page 169. If you have made mistakes, reread the article to gain a better understanding of it.

B. Look at the graph that accompanies this article, and answer these questions.

1. Is this a line graph, a bar graph or a pie-shaped graph?

2. Why is this shape of graph particularly suited to a report on basketball shoe sales?

3. a. Which company had the highest sales in 1990?
    b. What percent of the market did it have?

4. a. Which name brand was second?
    b. What percent of the market did it have?

5. How did Converse, the oldest company, do in 1990?

6. What is the source of this graph?

II. Expanding Your Vocabulary

A. Getting Meaning from Context

Use context clues to determine the meaning of each word, found in the paragraph indicated in parentheses. Choose the correct definition.

1. array (2):
    a. brightness
    b. varied group

2. niche (4):
    a. the place that a product occupies in a market
    b. a recessed area in a wall

3. saturation (5):
    a. striking of a target
    b. putting on the market as much of an item as can be sold

4. deny (11):
    a. say something isn't true
    b. to lie

5. quality (14):
    a. popularity
    b. excellence

6. breakthrough (16):
    a. removal of a restriction on a market
    b. new and major success on the market

7. paradigm (19):
    a. cause
    b. example or model

8. incorporates (24):
    a. becomes a corporation
    b. includes

9. tinker (26):
    a. change a great deal
    b. change in small ways

10. hype (28):
    a. exaggeration designed to sell
    b. a medium for selling

B. Working with Adjectives

Adjectives describe and add color to sentences. Complete the blanks with adjectives from the article. The numbers of the paragraphs for you to refer to are in parentheses.

1. _____ leathers (2)

2. _____ array of colors (2)

3. _____ cushioning devices (2)

4. _____ basketball player (8)

5. _____ majority of these shoes (13)

6. _____ play in a pickup game (20)

7. _____ bladder (24)

Write one or two sentences in which you describe high-style sneakers to someone who has never seen them. Use several adjectives.

III. Analyzing Paragraphs

Paragraphs 9 to 23 develop the comparison (similarities) and contrast (differences) in the marketing strategies of Nike and Reebok. Make a list below of some of the similarities and differences in marketing strategy that are stated in these paragraphs. The first few items have been provided for you.

Similarities:

Both Nike and Reebok spent about $130 million each

_____

_____

Differences:

Nike signed Michael Jordan

_____

_____

Reebok appealed to average players

_____

_____

Write your own sentence comparing the current styles of athletic shoe with those of their predecessors. (See paragraph 2.)

IV. Talking and Writing

Discuss the following topics. Then choose one of them to write about.

1. Much of this article discusses how advertising builds a market for a product. Does advertising cause you to buy particular products and brands?

2. Find an ad in a magazine or newspaper and analyze its appeal. To whom is it directed? Does it clearly make its appeal? Would you be persuaded to buy something by this ad?

3. Analyze the popularity of a product. Was it marketing or other factors that created its appeal?

FOCUS ON THE NEWSPAPER

Business

Analyzing Business Articles; Reading Stock Prices

The business section of a newspaper contains information that affects people's economic lives. Individuals with money to invest can find information and advice that will help them earn money on investments in stocks, bonds or real estate. Everyone can find information about employment trends and developing career areas. Since we live in a global economy, economic events in other countries that can affect business where you live are reported.

Topics of Business Articles

You will find a variety of articles in the business section, including:
- articles reporting the financial situation of companies, whether they are running at a profit or a loss
- articles reporting new products and technology developed or being developed by businesses, and how these might affect the businesses
- information on whether currencies, such as the dollar, are going up or down in value
- articles on how political policies and elections are affecting business

And the list could continue. All the articles help the reader analyze current business conditions.

Exercise 1: It's Your Business

Analyze a business article by answering these questions.

Analysis of a Business Article

1. What's the headline? How does it help you predict the content and viewpoint of the article? _____

2. What is the purpose of the article? (to report conditions of a company, new product, trends in the stock market, experts' opinion on economic conditions and so on) _____
_____

3. What is the main idea of the article? _____
_____

4. Does the article make a prediction about the future? If so, what is the prediction?
_____

5. Does the article give the reader any advice? If so, what is it? _____
_____

Exercise 2: The Language of Business

Like all areas, business uses its own special vocabulary. To understand business articles, you need to know terms such as *recession, bonds, stocks, futures, bull market.* Read two or three business articles. Write down at least five sentences that include words you don't know and underline the words. Discuss the terms in class and see if you can define them. Research terms that are not known.

Exercise 3: How's Business?

Scan the business section of newspapers over the past several weeks, looking for information about general business conditions in your area. As you read, look for answers to the following questions. Be prepared to discuss your conclusions with the class.

1. Is it difficult to find a job right now? Why? In what fields are employment opportunities best?
2. For the person with capital to invest, what is a good place to put it now, according to the experts?
3. What economic problems does your area face at this time?
4. What is the economic outlook—optimistic or pessimistic?

Reading Stock Prices

Daily newspapers run long lists of the stock and bond prices of companies on the major exchanges. Investors who own any of these stocks or bonds can follow the fluctuating prices in the daily paper.

Exercise 4: The Ups and Downs

In class, practice reading the newspaper listing of stock prices. Note some newspapers will provide a key to help you read the information. Then choose the stock of a well-known company on one of the major exchanges. "Purchase" 100 shares, and follow the closing price for any 4 days within a 2-week period. At the end of the two weeks, "sell" the stock. During the period that you "own" the stock, fill in the following information:

Name of stock purchased _____

Date of purchase _____ Price per share _____

Date: _____ Closing price: _____ Date: _____ Closing price: _____

Date: _____ Closing price: _____ Date: _____ Closing price: _____

Profit or loss (on 100 shares): _____

Do you know any reasons why the price went up or down?

Education

Education

New Under the Tree: Computers for Tots

Previewing the Article

Diane Bishop won't be getting her 2-year-old daughter a cuddly stuffed animal or a shiny red wagon this Christmas. Instead, Bishop is looking for the latest high-tech product for small children, a computer. This trend is so popular that a large New York toy store has added a new department, the Learning Center.

Ambitious mothers like Diane Bishop shop there for the equipment that they believe will give their children an advantage in early learning. But educators are not certain that these simple computer programs teach much of anything to the child. Will the flashing colors and "peppy" music excite toddlers about learning, or not? This article describes the computer programs being used by young children, and it examines the issues surrounding their value.

Before You Read

Before you read the article, discuss these questions.
1. How are children in your native culture educated in their early years?
2. Do you think that computers are a good gift for small children? Why, or why not?

As You Read

As you read, look for what a typical computer product for a preschooler is like, including its response to right and wrong answers.

New Under the Tree: Computers for Tots

By Carol Lawson
New York Times Service

NEW YORK—Diane Bishop looked tense. And confused.

There she was, in the midst of the Christmas rush, surrounded by the electronic beeps, clicks and flashing lights of the Learning Center on the second floor at F.A.O. Schwarz.

She was picking out a present for her daughter, Amanda. Actually, Ms. Bishop was in the famous toy store to select more than a present.

"You could call it a milestone," she said. "It will be right up there in Amanda's life with her first tooth, first bicycle and first airplane ride."

5   She was in the Learning Center to pick out Amanda's first computer.

Amanda is 2 years old. Like many children her age who can barely pronounce the word computer, she will wake up to find one under the tree Monday morning.

Computer makers are plugging into new territory. First they took on the office. Then they wired the home and the classroom. Now they are going after the playroom.

When Amanda Bishop was born, computers for preschoolers were barely a blip on the brain waves of computer designers. But all that has changed rapidly as computer manufacturers tuned into the anxieties of parents who want to program very young children for the path to Princeton.

Computers for preschoolers are essentially video games with an educational twist. They are designed to grab the attention of young minds with peppy electronic music and animated figures that look cute and move fast.

10   For example, press the letter S on the Fisher-Price Spelling Starter, and a

Karen Cheever

Very young children play with computer programs designed to help them learn basic reading and math skills at a tender age.

spider dances on the screen. Or press the number 4 on the Fisher-Price Math Starter, and four joggers spring across the screen.

The computers, which range in price from $20 to $200, feature programs that teach such rudimentary "subjects" as shapes, colors, numbers and letters. There also are more advanced programs that aim to teach spelling, reading, vocabulary and math.

"The goal is to prepare children for school and help them do better in the classroom," said Jon Campbell, media relations manager for Texas Instruments Inc., which this year added four new preschool computers to what it calls its EET line, or electronic educational toys.

Another goal is to help children make friends with computers. "They are going to live with computers their whole lives," Mr. Campbell said.

"The future for these products looks very good," he said. "There is a

growing emphasis on education, and parents and grandparents want to see their children get ahead."

15   The expanding preschool market includes electronic toys that, with their keyboards and display screens, look like miniature personal computers. There also is an array of educational software that can be used with the parents' more sophisticated home computer.

The products come in boxes with the word "educational" stamped on them. They are packaged with the promise of being "easy to use," "friendly," and "fun."

Fisher-Price's software that "teaches number recognition" to children as young as 3, comes with the message: "No previous computer experience necessary."

Subjects are taught through the presentation of questions or problems. Children register their answers by pushing a button.

The makers of this merchandise

endorse the theory of child-rearing that says youngsters learn by positive reinforcement. Right answers are usually greeted with a burst of upbeat electronic fanfare.

20 The Socrates Touch Pad signals correct responses with an applauding robot. Texas Instruments' Speak and Read talks back, exclaiming, "You're right! Great!"

Wrong answers elicit an electronic dirge or an empathetic voice that says, "Wrong answer. Try again."

Some experts take a dim view of encouraging very young children to learn with computers. They say that parents and other adults, not to mention old-fashioned books, can do the job just as well.

Ms. Bishop would not hear of it. "My daughter is applying to nursery school," she said. "Maybe this will give her an edge."

After nearly two hours of pushing buttons and trying to become computer-literate on the preschool level, Ms. Bishop made her choice.

25 For $45 she bought My Little Computer, made by Texas Instruments. Designed for children aged 2 to 6, it has simple programs that teach matching skills and multiple choice as well as more advanced programs for learning numbers, letters, spelling, counting and names of animals.

Some educators say that though preschoolers might have fun with these computers, they do not necessarily

learn from them. Another objection is the introduction of academic stress so early in life.

"We have to recognize that computers are a fact of life, but I am concerned that these toys are putting too much pressure on children at too young an age," said Barbara A. Willer, a former preschool teacher and the public affairs director of the National Association for the Education of Young Children.

"There is an overemphasis on the memorization of letters and numbers," she said. "Parents think they are precursors of later learning, of higher scores. But children who are not ready to gain those skills may become turned off to learning or convinced they are dumb."

I. Getting the Message

A. After reading the article, choose the best answer for each item.

1. This article suggests that computers for very young children were designed with
   a. children's creativity in mind
   b. the support of educators
   c. the anxiety of parents in mind

2. Diane Bishop thinks that Amanda's new computer will
   a. give Amanda an advantage in nursery school
   b. teach Amanda multiplication
   c. be very expensive

3. Computers for toddlers are similar to
   a. video games
   b. television
   c. office computers

4. Some educators believe that the preschool computers overemphasize
   a. peppy music and animated figures
   b. memorization of letters and numbers
   c. pushing buttons

Check your answers with the key on page 169. If you have made mistakes, reread the article to gain a better understanding of it.

B. Find the phrase that doesn't fit into each category.

1. *sounds a preschool computer makes*

| beeps and clicks | peppy electronic music | animated figures | applause |

2. *positive reinforcement*

| applauding robots | matching skills | "You're right!" | "Great!" |

3. *skills taught on preschool computers*

| names of animals | creation of stories | memorization | numbers |

■ II. Expanding Your Vocabulary

A. Getting Meaning from Context

Use context clues to determine the meaning of each word, found in the paragraph indicated in parentheses. Choose the correct definition.

1. tense (1):   a. nervous   b. confident
2. peppy (9):   a. lively   b. sad
3. twist (9):   a. spiraling movement   b. unexpected characteristic
4. miniature (15):   a. something less important   b. a model of reduced size
5. register (18):   a. explain   b. record
6. endorse (19):   a. give approval or support   b. sign
7. objection (26):   a. a statement of opposition b. response
8. stress (26):   a. emphasis   b. pressure

B. Reading for Suggested Meanings

Answer these questions.

1. In paragraph 8, the author suggests that parents who purchase computers for preschoolers want to program their children for *the path to* Princeton, a famous university in the United States. What is the hope of these parents?

2. In paragraph 11, the early-learning computers teach *rudimentary* subjects. Is the level of skills sophisticated or relatively simple?

3. Paragraph 19 talks of *positive reinforcement.*
   a. How do most people feel when they get *positive reinforcement*?
   b. How does a *burst of upbeat electronic fanfare* support positive reinforcement?

4. In paragraph 21, wrong answers result in an electronic *dirge.*
   a. What is a dirge?
   b. What does its use suggest here?

■ III. Working with Idioms

Study the meanings of these idioms and expressions.

pick out (3) = choose

find under the tree (6) = be given as a Christmas present

barely a blip on the brain waves (8) = hardly a thought in the mind

tuned into (8) = alert to

grab the attention of (9) = gain the interest of

get ahead (14) = succeed

take a dim view of (22) = look on negatively

give an edge (23) = help to gain an advantage

turned off to (28) = no longer interested in

Complete these sentences, using the idioms and expressions.

1. Diane Bishop plans to _____ a computer to give to her daughter. She hopes that the computer will _____ to her daughter in nursery school.

2. Many educators _____ computers for young children. They are afraid that children may become _____ learning if they are forced to learn basic skills at too early an age.

3. The electronic beeps and flashing lights of the computer games _____ young children.

IV. Making Sense of Sentences

This article presents the viewpoint of computer makers and Ms. Bishop, who are for (*pro*) preschool computers, and some educators who are against (*anti*) computers. List two sentences from the article that support each of the opposing views.

Pro	Anti
1. _____	1. _____
2. _____	2. _____

Make up a sentence of your own that expresses your opinion about buying computers for toddlers.

V. Talking and Writing

Discuss the following topics. Then choose one of them to write about.

1. Do you believe that toddlers are benefited by computers? Why, or why not?

2. Are parents like Bishop too ambitious for their children?

3. What is an early educational memory that you have? It can have occurred inside or outside of school.

4. How should parents prepare their children to succeed in school?

Education

Moscow Chefs: Where's the Beef?

Previewing the Article

"Necessity is the mother of invention," a proverb says. To learn to be a chef in a Moscow cooking school, one certainly must be inventive.

While cooking schools in most countries pride themselves on fresh ingredients and creative recipes, Moscow cooking students at PTS No. 41 must satisfy themselves with the best model food that the country has to offer. This article explains how Moscow students are coping with learning to cook without all the necessary ingredients. This is the case because of food shortages at a time when Russia is moving from communism toward a market economy. However, hope and a new exchange program with a cooking school in Paris may help these future Russian chefs survive the meatless Moscow months.

Before You Read

Before you read the article, discuss these questions.
1. Do you think it is possible to learn a skill like driving, cooking or swimming without doing it yourself? Why, or why not?
2. Have you ever taken cooking lessons or known someone who has? Describe the experience.

As You Read

As you read, look for answers to this question: What methods are used to teach Russian students cooking?

Moscow Chefs: Where's the Beef?

© WOLFGANG KAEHLER 1993.

Professional cooks preparing traditional Russian cuisine—students look forward to the day when they can work with real food.

By Eleanor Randolph
Washington Post Service

MOSCOW—Larisa Tatarskaya is standing in front of a class of Russian teenagers, mostly males, explaining how to cook something few in this country have seen: steak.

She is holding what looks like a nice cut of meat, except that a real piece of sirloin would have slipped off the platter and onto a student's desk.

The steak here in one of Moscow's largest cooking schools is actually a slab of wax, one of a huge assortment of fake-food platters around the classroom. Neat mounds of olive-green peas, translucent fish, a pile of roasted potatoes, brown crispy-looking onions—they are all synthetic dishes used as teaching tools at Professional Technical School No. 41.

In a nation where food is scarce, how do you learn to cook? Mostly by the book. How do you learn what a good meal looks like? Make it look like this wax model.

5 "What is the role of the fat in the frying pan?" Tatarskaya is asking her students, all dressed in fashionable jeans and Western jackets. A full-bodied young man stands to answer. "It evens out the temperature between the meat and the pan," he recites.

Tatarskaya nods, pointing to a plate with a wax steak in the middle, explaining the chemical reactions in the meat and talking about how this steak does not have to be fried bloodless because "the English" like their meat with a little pink part on the inside.

At PTS No. 41, the 600 students are learning how to be professional cooks in a society where—for the last 70 years—food has been viewed more as fuel for human workers than as something to be savored and enjoyed. Their course is a grim lesson in how to cook what isn't there.

To be sure, food from a factory kitchen nearby is occasionally available, and there are knives and stoves and potato-peeling machines at the ready in the basement kitchen when it appears. There are also apprenticeships at restaurants. But by Western cooking school standards, most of the study of how to prepare a dinner is theoretical.

As a result some of the new chefs in Moscow tend to avoid those trained in the old Soviet way. As Bernard Derroisne, the French chef at TrenMos, a successful U.S.–Soviet joint-venture restaurant, puts it: "I might just as well hire people off the street as from these schools. They have to learn everything all over again, and I have to be the teacher for them. The most important thing is that they have a desire to learn."

10 Derroisne says the key talent for a professional chef in Moscow is "learning to substitute." There are days when he has to make cheesecake without cream cheese, he says. Baking powder is sometimes available, sometimes not.

At PTS No. 41, however, the idea of teaching how to cook what's here is too distressing. Instead, they learn the ideal, like learning by the book how to drive a car that one may never have.

Faced with such problems, what saves PTS No. 41 is the principal, a jovial, red-haired woman named Liubov Fedorovna Klokune. Klokune, a mathematics teacher who loves to cook as a hobby, spends her time trying to rise above the scarcity that dominates Russian cuisine in this period. Her method, she says, is to teach cooking with the presumption that someday her students will be able to walk into the *gastronom* and buy potatoes, leeks, meat, flour and ginger root to the specifications of a favorite recipe.

As it is now, most cooks go to the stores first, buy what's there and then decide what can be made for dinner. "We teach students what it should be," Klokune says. "If we started with what is in our stores, we would have to throw the textbooks away."

Klokune, who recently began an exchange program with a cooking school in Paris, has also begun trying to give her students a larger and tastier repertoire. An apple torte made in France can be made here, she said. There are apples in the private markets. Flour and sugar, although scarce, are sometimes available. Lemons are plentiful but expensive. Butter and milk can be found if one is patient. During one of the occasional cooking sessions, the students made the torte. "They thought it was delicious," she said.

15 After visiting the school on one of the many days when food was not available, we were invited back to see what happened when it was. In the basement, students were clustered around long tables that held a few carrots, a few beets and a few pieces of dry-looking meat. The 16 students wore clean white uniforms complete with chefs hats that ranged from a small puff of cloth to a sailor's cap.

"Today we are doing salads and cold dishes," explained Klokune.

Some students chopped the carrots and cooked beets; others seemed to spend the entire time watching. There seemed to be some unspoken decision about who got to touch the food—the better the student, the closer he comes to the actual carrot. One student—who saw the Westerners' cameras and began to perform for them immediately the way students do everywhere—introduced himself as "the best chef in the school" and announced that his specialty was pizza. His colleagues smirked or snickered. He had plenty of time for such antics since he was not allowed to touch the food. "He's really the worst student," whispered Klokune.

One of the better students worked quietly and then proudly displayed his work. In a small container were beets, carrots, potatoes and chopped eggs.

From across the room came the teacher, shouting as he moved toward the table. "You know better than that," he hissed. "You put the egg next to the potatoes. The egg never goes with the potatoes. You know better than that. Go over there. Go help them cook the vegetables." The boy skulked away to another section of the basement.

20 Although technical schools are often considered the lowest rank in the educational system, PTS No. 41 has virtues that none of the others can claim, Klokune said as we walked from the kitchen and upstairs in the huge, old brick building.

"We have great teachers here," she smiled, "and all those wax models, we are lucky to have them. Most were made 20 years ago and the factory no longer does this kind of thing."

Klokune, like many high school principals, is a cheerleader for her institution. "No other cooking school can get them," she said proudly. "That is why the level of training here is higher than at the other cooking schools in Moscow. We are the best."

I. Getting the Message

A. After reading the article, indicate if each statement is true (*T*) or false (*F*).

_____ 1. PTS No. 41 is Moscow's oldest cooking school.

_____ 2. For 70 years in the former Soviet Union, there has been general indifference to fine cuisine.

_____ 3. New foreign chefs in Moscow tend to seek students trained in the Soviet way.

_____ 4. The practical approach to menu planning in Moscow is determined by what foods are available.

_____ 5. If Klokune followed the practical approach, she would throw the textbooks away.

_____ 6. The better the cooking student, the less he or she comes in contact with real food.

_____ 7. The graduates of the cooking school lack firsthand experience in cooking.

Check your answers with the key on page 169. If you have made mistakes, reread the article to gain a better understanding of it.

B. Answer the following questions.

1. What basic problem does the cooking school have?
2. What is the solution to the problem?
3. What is the problem with the solution?

II. Expanding Your Vocabulary

Getting Meaning from Context

Use context clues to determine the meaning of each word, found in the paragraphs indicated in parentheses. Choose the correct definition.

1. actually (3):   a. currently   b. really
2. synthetic (3):   a. real   b. artificial
3. grim (7):   a. depressing   b. unexpected
4. apprenticeships (8): a. jobs   b. instruction in a trade
5. ideal (11):   a. something existing only   b. ways to be creative
                              in thought
6. distressing (11):   a. upsetting   b. appealing
7. clustered (15):   a. grouped close together   b. placed in ordered rows
8. virtues (20):   a. advantages   b. courage

III. Working with Idioms

Study the meanings of these idioms and expressions.

by the book (4) = closely following the written instructions

the role of (5) = the purpose of

even out (5) = equalize

to be sure (8) = certainly, of course

at the ready (8) = available

rise above (12) = overcome a problem

that range from . . . to . . . (15) = that include

Answer these questions.

1. In paragraph 4, what is the humor or double meaning involved in learning to cook *by the book*?
2. In paragraph 5, how does the student explain *the role of* fat in cooking?
3. In paragraph 8, what is *at the ready* for the time when food will appear?
4. In paragraph 12, what helps Klokune *rise above* the food scarcity in Russian cuisine?

IV. Analyzing Paragraphs

Reread the paragraphs indicated. Choose the answer that best completes each sentence.

1. Paragraphs 1 to 3 do all but
   a. introduce the limits of the Russian cooking school
   b. develop an example of how cooking is taught
   c. introduce the main character

2. In paragraphs 9 and 10, Bernard Derroisne is introduced for all but the following reason:
   a. to comment on Moscow-trained chefs
   b. to explain joint-ventures
   c. to comment on the scarcity of food in Moscow today

3. Paragraphs 11, 12 and 13 contrast all but one of the following:
   a. learning about the ideal vs. the reality of cooking in Moscow
   b. basing a menu on what is available vs. a cookbook recipe
   c. cooking Russian vs. French cuisine

4. In paragraphs 20, 21 and 22, the tone conveyed by Klokune is
   a. hopelessness
   b. optimism mixed with irony
   c. anger

V. Talking and Writing

Discuss the following topics. Then choose one of them to write about.

1. The cooking school at PTS No. 41 provides an example of how the problems of a culture limit its ability to provide up-to-date education. Yet the faculty and students enrolled at PTS No. 41 are doing the best that they can under difficult circumstances. Do you believe that their experience will be helpful or harmful to them? Explain.

2. Have you ever taken lessons in a field that requires practice or training? Describe your experience.

Education

*For Japanese, Cramming for Exams Starts Where the
Cradle Leaves Off*

Previewing the Article

Every society must deal with the important question of how best to educate
its children. In recent years, worldwide attention has been focused on
Japanese educational methods because of (1) the high level of academic
achievement they attain and (2) concern that intense academic competition
may be harming Japanese students. This article examines the pros and
cons of a highly competitive system that begins cramming information into
children during early childhood.

Before You Read

Before you read the article, discuss these questions.
1. How would you evaluate the academic environment you were educated in? Was there too much competition and pressure to succeed
   or not enough? Did the system teach students to love learning or to
   fear it?
2. In your opinion, at what age are children ready for academic competition involving tests, grades and selection based upon ability?

As You Read

As you read, look for the arguments for and against Japanese *jukus* (cram
schools). Also, try to determine if the author is presenting a totally objective
account of the system, or if he either favors or opposes jukus.

For Japanese, Cramming for Exams Starts Where the Cradle Leaves Off

By Steven R. Weisman
New York Times Service

TOKYO—Like many Japanese, Naoto Eguchi feels relentless pressure to get ahead. Rising at dawn, he works a full day with his regular colleagues and another three hours each evening in special study sessions. He then does a couple of hours of work at home before going to bed at midnight.

It is a heavy burden for an 11-year-old.

Naoto's immediate goal is to pass the entrance examinations for a private junior high school, a crucial step for eventual admission to a prestigious university. But he is already thinking about the future.

"My goal is to get a good job with a good company," he said.

5 The struggle to succeed in one of the world's most competitive societies is starting earlier and earlier, and nowhere is it more evident than in the growing popularity of cram schools that train students for examinations for private schools and colleges.

Once on the fringe of the system, cram schools, or *jukus,* are so pervasive and time-consuming in Japan that, especially for the elite, they have begun to function as a kind of shadow educational system, supplanting regular schools in importance for parents and students and reaching down to 2- and 3-year-old children.

The rise of jukus is praised as one of the secrets of Japanese success, a healthy reflection of a system of advancement based on merit. It is also criticized as a movement forcing a new generation to surrender its childhood out of an obsession with status and getting ahead.

"Jukus are harmful to Japanese education and to children," said Ikuo Amano, professor of sociology at the University of Tokyo. "It's not healthy for kids to have so little free time. It is not healthy to become completely caught up in competition and status at such a young age."

Recently, the Yano Research Institute found that nearly 4.4 million students were enrolled in some 50,000 to 60,000 jukus. That represents 18.6 percent of elementary school children and 52.2 percent of students in seventh through ninth grades. Japanese spent $10.9 billion on tutoring and cram schools last year, according to the institute, including $9 billion on jukus for students in the ninth grade or below—almost double the figure spent seven years ago.

10 The people who run and teach at jukus say the schools are popular only because they work, creating a lively and interesting environment in which students learn because they are enjoying themselves.

One of the most prestigious cram schools for 2- and 3-year-olds, Shingakai Juku, sends most of its pre-kindergarten graduates to prestigious elementary schools. If these students get good grades in a prestigious school, they can advance all the way to a university without having to take examinations.

"We really don't push knowledge on them," said Kigen Fujimoto, head of a branch of this juku in northwest Tokyo. "We are interested in teaching them how to play and enjoy learning."

In a nearby class, eight children, each about 3, sat politely in little chairs in a row as a teacher held up pictures of a kite, a dragon, and other objects, calling on the students to identify them.

"What is this shape?" she then said, holding up first a square, a triangle, and then a circle.

15 Several mothers who were waiting to pick up their children, expressed anxiety about subjecting their youngsters to such pressure. But they reasoned that it would be worth it if their children got into private schools early and did not have to worry about passing examinations later on.

"It's not an ideal thing to send your kids to such a place," said one mother, asking not to be identified for fear of criticism from other parents. She said she thought that her daughter was having a good time in this school, but continued, "If I told you I wasn't thinking about entrance examinations, I would be lying."

Juku teachers and administrators say that because their schools are profit-making enterprises, they have to guarantee results to succeed. The results are easy to measure, because they depend on how many graduates pass the examinations for private school.

The "examination hell" inflicted on children is widely criticized in Japan. In a recent survey, two-thirds of parents said competitive examinations were their worst problem in raising children. But parents are also eager to give their children every advantage.

"Jukus are playing on the status anxieties of these parents," said Makoto Oda, an author who taught in jukus in Tokyo for more than 20 years. "All parents are absolutely terrified that their children will fall behind."

20 Juku defenders say that students are only gaining the discipline and ability to withstand pressure that they will need in life.

But the very success of jukus in training youngsters to pass exams has made the competition worse: jukus help more students pass exams, so the exams have to be made more difficult.

"Jukus are raising a generation of kids who can only pass entrance examinations," said Hiroyuki Tsukamoto, an official of the Japan Teachers Union. "But the most important educational purpose is giving children the ability to live in society. That's being left out."

The Education Ministry has tried to combat the juku system by improving public schools, reducing class sizes, upgrading teacher training, and making the curriculum more flexible. But ministry officials acknowledge that those steps have not worked.

I. Getting the Message

A. After reading the article, choose the best answer for each item.

1. In Japan, jukus have been established primarily to help
   a. students who are having difficulty keeping up with their schoolwork
   b. preschool children whose parents are poor and uneducated
   c. students of all ages whose parents want them to do well on competitive exams

2. The author of this article seems to
   a. approve of jukus
   b. disapprove of jukus
   c. have no opinion about jukus

3. Jukus are owned and operated by
   a. Japanese parents
   b. the Education Ministry of the Japanese public school system
   c. private individuals who make a profit

4. Most Japanese parents and educators would agree that
   a. the Japanese educational system puts a lot of pressure on students
   b. Japan has the best educational system in the world
   c. jukus should be established in other countries with weak educational programs

5. Jukus are available to
   a. all Japanese students
   b. those who can afford the high tuition
   c. those who score well on exams

Check your answers with the key on page 169. If you have made mistakes, reread the article to gain a better understanding of it.

B. Some parents and educators would disapprove of Naoto Eguchi's schedule, which is described in paragraph 1. What are three possible criticisms of the life-style of this 11-year-old?

II. Expanding Your Vocabulary

A. Getting Meaning from Context

Use context clues to determine the meaning of each word or phrase, found in the paragraph indicated in parentheses. Choose the correct definition.

1. colleagues (1):
   a. companions at school or work
   b. rivals at school or work

2. immediate goal (3):
   a. important goal
   b. short-term goal

3. a prestigious school (3, 11):
   a. a school that generally accepts only those students with high academic ratings
   b. a school that accepts any student who applies

4. pervasive (6):
   a. difficult
   b. found in many places

5. fringe (6):
   a. outside the cultural mainstream; a minor part of
   b. strips of fabric used for decoration

6. status (7, 8, 19):   a. grade in school   b. position in society
7. upgrading (23):   a. training to teach at the b. improving
                                  secondary rather than
                                  elementary level

B. Reading for Suggested Meanings

Answer these questions.

1. In paragraph 6, the word *jukus* is translated as cram schools. Does *cram* mean to put in too much or too little?

2. In paragraph 7, is *obsession* something that a person thinks about occasionally or all the time?

3. In paragraphs 15, 16 and 19, the author talks about Japanese parents.
    a. What emotion is mentioned in all three paragraphs?
    b. Could that emotion explain why parents haven't insisted upon changes in the educational system? Why?

4. According to paragraph 21, "successful" jukus have forced test writers to make the exams more difficult. Why did this happen? What is the purpose of the tests?

III. Working with Idioms

Study the meanings of these idioms and expressions.

Phrasal verbs:

leave off (headline) = end, stop

get ahead (1) = succeed

become caught up in (8) = get very involved in

pick up (15) = get someone or something from a place

fall behind (19) = not do as well as others in the group

be left out (22) = be omitted, not included

Other expressions:

the cradle (headline) = the period of infancy

cram (headline) = try to learn a lot of information in a short time (usually for a test)

work (10, 23) = be effective

Complete these sentences, using the idioms and expressions. Be sure to use the correct verb tense.

1. In Japan, even young children think about their future and want to _____ in the world.

2. Officials hoped that recent changes in the Japanese public school system would decrease the popularity of jukus, but this plan has not _____.

3. Japanese mothers waited outside the classroom to _____ their young children.

4. Some people say that in the Japanese educational system social skills are _____.

5. If students always have to _____ for tests, they may never develop a love of knowledge for its own sake.

IV. Focusing on Style and Tone

A. *Appreciating Elements of Effective Style*

Answer these questions.

1. In paragraph 2, the author gives Naoto's story a surprising twist.
   a. In paragraph 1, what do we assume about Naoto Eguchi?
   b. What do we find out in paragraph 2?

2. In general, a direct quotation emphasizes a statement more than an indirect quotation does. In paragraph 4, the author uses a direct quotation. Why, in this situation, is this familiar statement surprising?

3. Paragraph 12 quotes a head of a juku saying, "We are interested in teaching them [the children] how to play and enjoy themselves." What is the ironic contrast that follows in paragraph 13?

B. *Noting Negative Connotations*

To emphasize a negative feeling about jukus, the author has used many words with negative connotations. In each pair listed, choose the word or phrase that seems more negative to you.

1. hell / heaven   4. cram / study

2. obsession / thought   5. replacing / supplanting

3. persistent / relentless

Reread the article. Which of the words from each pair do you find there?

V. Talking and Writing

Discuss the following topics. Then choose one of them to write about.

1. To some extent, all parents face the same problem as the Japanese parents described in this article. All parents want their children to get a good education. Yet, no parent wants to deprive his or her child of an enjoyable, anxiety-free childhood. What advice can you give to help parents decide how much pressure is too much? Is the child's reaction any clue?

2. Looking back on your childhood, do you think you were pushed too hard or not enough? How did the attitudes of your teachers and parents affect how hard you tried? How did those attitudes affect your accomplishments?

3. Note that jukus are expensive. What does that suggest about their effect upon Japanese education?

4. Compare and contrast Japanese jukus to your native country's methods of preparing students for higher education.

Education

What's in a Gesture? Kids Need to Learn

Previewing the Article

Nonverbal reading—does it sound impossible? Actually, you do it all the time. You "read" (receive messages from) the gestures, facial expressions, posture and tone of voice of people you're talking to.

"That kind of reading is instinctive," you may say. "Everyone knows how to read a smile, a hug or an enthusiastic handshake." Not so. Some children must be taught to "read" nonverbal communication. This article explains how the learning problem is being diagnosed and treated.

Before You Read

Before you read, discuss these questions.
1. What are the differences between gestures, facial expressions and posture? What are some examples of nonverbal messages communicated in each of these ways?

2. Of course, some nonverbal signals vary from one culture to another. What are some gestures you know that have a specific meaning in your native society? Do you think people from other countries understand them?

As You Read

As you read, look for reasons why misreading nonverbal messages creates problems.

What's in a Gesture? Kids Need to Learn

By Daniel Goleman
New York Times Service

UNPOPULARITY, poor grades and a host of other problems that afflict children may derive from an inability to read the nonverbal messages of teachers and peers, new findings show.

The results are based on a test that measures nonverbal skills: reading the emotions that are revealed in tone of voice, for instance, and sensing how close to stand while talking to someone. It is the first such test designed specifically for use with children.

The test assesses ability to read nonverbal messages in several ways. For instance, a child watches 40 slides of children and adults, rating their expressions as happy, sad, angry and so on. The same is done with slides showing various postures and gestures, and with audiotapes of various tones of voice.

The child's ability to sense nonverbal messages is also measured more actively.

5   In one test, he or she is videotaped while making an expression to communicate the emotion for a hypothetical situation, like receiving a long-wanted birthday present. In other tests, the child is told to use only hands and arms to communicate a particular emotion or to read a sentence in ways that express a variety of emotions.

Studies of more than 1,000 children aged 9 to 11 showed that those who scored lowest on the test tended to be among the least popular in their class. They also tended to do less well academically, even though their intelligence was just as high on average.

The studies found that up to 10 percent of all children may have problems with nonverbal communication severe enough to impair their social or academic functioning. When trying to make friends, they are typically unable to approach other children without putting them off, and they often unwittingly respond to teachers in ways that get them in trouble.

The test will allow screening of children to identify such deficiencies. Psychologists believe that helping the children improve those skills may save them from serious setbacks in later life.

Since most emotional messages between people are communicated nonverbally—by a gesture or tone of voice, say—the inability to read or send such messages adeptly is a major social handicap, said Stephen Nowicki, a psychologist at Emory University in Atlanta, who developed the scale.

10   "Because they are unware of the messages they are sending, or misinterpret how other children are feeling," he said, "unpopular children may not even realize that they are initiating many of the negative reactions they receive from their peers."

Unpopular children may inadvertently communicate over-eagerness that their peers misinterpret as aggression, according to a study published by Dr. Nowicki and Carolyn Oxenford this year in The Journal of Genetic Psychology.

Among the problems common in children lacking nonverbal skills, Dr. Nowicki said, is a continual sense of frustration that can lead to depression or apathy.

"They get rebuffed and don't know why," Dr. Nowicki said. "In essence, they just don't understand what's going on. They may think they're acting happy but actually appear to others too excited or even angry. They are mystified when other kids are angry in return."

Such children develop a sense that they have little or no control over how people treat them, Dr. Nowicki found. By extension, they feel they lack control over their fate in general. Other research has shown that this attitude leads to a defeatism that undermines children emotionally.

15   "They look emotionally disturbed, anxious, depressed, angry," said Dr. Nowicki. "But something else is going on. The anger and such don't come from family conflict or other typical sources of emotional disturbance in children. It's an effect of being poor at reading nonverbal messages. If you teach them to do it correctly, the signs of emotional disturbance disappear."

Dr. Nowicki believes that the problem is a learning disability, akin to reading problems. Because the language of emotion is nonverbal, skill at reading such messages is crucial for psychological adjustment.

"If a child makes consistent errors in using nonverbal language, such as standing too close when talking to someone or talking too loud or soft," said Dr. Nowicki, "other children will see them as strange and to be avoided."

In one approach, children are trained to read facial expressions. They begin by watching videotapes of expressions and try to tell if the faces are expressing different feelings. Once they are able to distinguish expressions, they try to express those same feelings themselves. The children are videotaped, then shown what they are doing right or wrong.

Finally, the children try out what they have learned in a controlled situation, showing what they would do, for example, if they met another child they would like to make friends with.

20   "We've tried the training with 150 children so far, and the results have been quite positive," said Dr. Nowicki, adding that some children have become markedly better at making friends and getting along with their teachers.

I. Getting the Message

A. After reading the article, indicate if each statement is true (*T*) or false (*F*).

_____ 1. This article tells about researchers who were interested in finding children with a particular learning problem and then helping them to overcome it.

_____ 2. Children taking the nonverbal test tried to interpret the messages of others and also tried to send messages with gestures and facial expressions.

_____ 3. Children with nonverbal "reading" problems tend to be less intelligent than students without this problem.

_____ 4. Children with nonverbal "reading" problems tend to get lower grades in school than the other students.

_____ 5. The problem described in the article is a learning disability that can be treated with some success.

_____ 6. People use nonverbal communication more often to convey information than to convey emotions.

Check your answers with the key on page 169. If you have made mistakes, reread the article to gain a better understanding of it.

B. Read the following list of behaviors. Identify with a *V* each one that sends a verbal message and with an *N* each one that sends a nonverbal message. (Remember, a verbal message involves words.)

_____ 1. crying   _____ 4. using slang
_____ 2. asking for help   _____ 5. applauding
_____ 3. slamming a door   _____ 6. shaking your fist

II. Expanding Your Vocabulary

A. Getting Meaning from Context

Use context clues to determine the meaning of each word or phrase, found in the paragraph indicated in parentheses. Choose the correct definition.

1. host (1):   a. someone who has guests   b. a great deal of

2. slides (3):   a. playground equipment to slide down   b. photographs that can be shown on a wall or screen

3. like (5):   a. such as, similar to   b. enjoy, prefer

4. tended to be/do (6):   a. it happened occasionally   b. it usually happened

5. screening (8):   a. putting a screen on a window or door   b. separating one group from another

6. setbacks (8):   a. reversals in progress   b. depression

7. scale (9):   a. a machine used to determine weight   b. a series of marks along a line, used to measure

8. positive (20):   a. successful   b. indicating the presence of a disease

B. *Using Negative Prefixes*

There are many negative prefixes in English. You'll find these examples in this reading: *dis-, im-, in-, non-* and *un-*. You'll also find the prefix *mis-*, which means wrong. Put the correct prefix before each word listed. Then discuss the meanings of the words.

1. _____ advertently
2. _____ aware
3. _____ interpret

4. _____ popular
5. _____ verbal
6. _____ wittingly

Two different word parts can be used before *ability*. Which ones? Discuss the meanings of the words.

_____ ability

_____ ability

III. Making Sense of Sentences

A. *Writing Noun Clauses with* That

In many sentences in this article, *that* introduces a noun clause that is the object of the verb. To study examples of this type of sentence, reread the first sentences in paragraphs 6, 7, 10 and 16. Then complete the following sentences with ideas from the article.

1. Dr. Nowicki probably hopes that _____.
2. The research described in this article showed that _____.

B. *Writing Adjective Clauses with* That

Sometimes clauses beginning with *that* are adjective clauses that describe the preceding noun. In the first sentence of this article, *that afflict children* is an adjective clause describing the word *problems*. Other examples are in paragraphs 2 and 14. Complete the adjective clauses with information from the article.

1. Children that _____ tend to be unpopular.
2. The researchers used a test that _____.

IV. Talking and Writing

Discuss these topics. Then choose one of them to write about.

1. In the society you are living in now, what are some examples of polite and impolite nonverbal behavior?
2. Have you ever had a problem because you misread a nonverbal message? Tell what happened.

FOCUS ON THE NEWSPAPER

Education

Analyzing Educational Issues and Articles;
Reading Educational Ads

"U.S. Educators Give President a Mixed 'Report Card,'" "Government Redefines Vocational Training": these are headlines you might find in the newspaper. Almost daily, newspapers carry articles about local, national and international issues in education. Covering topics ranging from the new educational products for tots to trends in employment retraining for adults, education articles are typically found on the news pages. Some papers publish special educational supplements several times a year. In addition to describing the latest in education news, these supplements have advertisements from colleges, universities, educational camps and other schools so that the reader can be informed of educational possibilities.

Issues in Education Articles

Often education articles hit the newspaper when there is a problem or an issue of some sort. Here are some typical ones:

- How is our national educational system doing? Are the scores and knowledge of current students declining compared with those of ten or twenty years ago?

- What is being done by the government to address problems with the educational system and to improve it?

- Are students being adequately trained to deal with the world of work?

- What groups in society have access to education, for example, to higher education?

- Are traditional classroom practices being changed?

- What are new trends in education in other countries?

  These are all issues that make an education topic appear on the news pages.

Exercise 1: Find the Issues

Look back over recent newspapers to find articles that deal with education. Identify the issue that each addresses. Can you find a pattern of what educational issues are currently being debated?

Exercise 2: Learn All About It

Analyze an education article by answering these questions.

Analysis of an Education Article

1. What's the headline? What key words helped you predict the content of the article?
    _____

2. What is the purpose of the article? (to report a problem in education, a new govern-
    ment policy, a new way of teaching and so on) _____

3. What is the main idea of the article? _____
    _____

4. Does the article report a problem? If so, what is it? _____
    _____

    Does the article offer a solution(s) to the problem. If so, what is it? _____
    _____

5. Does the article make you feel optimistic or pessimistic about this topic in education?
    Why? _____

Educational Advertising

Newspapers often have ads for schools. You can find out what schools
offer courses and diplomas you are interested in.

Exercise 3: Looking at Education Ads

Look at the ads below from the *International Herald Tribune*. Imagine
that you are interested in attending a school, and answer the questions.

1. What school would interest the more advanced student?

2. What is the chief benefit of the MBA program?/the diploma program?

3. Compose a brief letter requesting information about one of the programs.

Arts & Leisure

Arts and Leisure

Food for Luck: New Year's Rituals

Previewing the Article

A part of almost everyone's leisure time is spent celebrating holidays. The arrival of the new year is a holiday around the world. From one culture to another, New Year's customs vary, but they also have much in common, as the following article shows.

Human beings are probably the only animals that worry and wonder about their futures. Many people want to know the future and even control it. This article shows how people around the world have tried to influence coming events through their New Year's menus.

Does the title of the article, "Food for Luck," remind you of another saying? It's a variation of the saying *food for thought*, which means *something worth thinking about.*

Before You Read

Before you read the article, discuss these questions.
1. What are some of the New Year's customs celebrated in your culture? Do some of them involve food? Do some of them involve predicting or controlling the future?
2. What superstitions do you know about acquiring good luck and avoiding bad luck?

As You Read

As you read, look for the reasons why various foods eaten at the start of the new year are considered lucky.

Will the foods mentioned in this article really bring you good luck? Maybe—and maybe not. But here's one safe prediction: If you eat all of them on New Year's Eve, you'll begin the new year with a stomachache.

Food for Luck: New Year's Rituals

By Dena Kleiman
New York Times Service

NEW YORK—The notion of eating foods to change one's fortune dates to ancient Babylonia and the world's first known recipes, according to Nan Rothschild, professor of anthropology at Barnard College.

"To say that a food brings good luck is a way of controlling the environment and one's destiny," Rothchild said.

It is especially at the beginning of each new year that many societies rely

The symbols are simplistic and the aspirations revolve around personal gain, abundance and health.

on certain foods that are thought to possess magical powers. In the southern United States, for example, one popular New Year's dish is a casserole of rice and black-eyed peas known as Hoppin' John, a name of unknown origin.

The dish is said to bring prosperity although few are sure why. Some theorize that a little of this concoction goes a long way and that those who eat it on New Year's Day will not go hungry.
5   In Italy, many people make a ritual out of eating lentils. In Greece, families bake a special bread, vasilopita, and bury a coin inside it. "Whoever finds the coin will be wealthy," explains Diane Kochilas, author of "The Food and Wine of Greece" (St. Martin's Press).

In Japan, people eat long noodles. In Spain, the custom is to eat 12 individual grapes in the seconds leading up to the New Year. In India, revelers eat fudge.

What ties these New Year's talismans together is the seemingly universal notion that what one does and what one eats during those first delicate hours of the New Year will determine everything that will follow.

"It is as if we are reborn with the New Year and that whatever you do

on that first day will affect what you do the rest of the year," said Jack Santino, a professor of folklore and popular culture at Bowling Green University in Ohio.

Santino said that in Bowling Green, a rural community where families are largely of German descent, the New Year's tradition is sauerkraut and pork.
10   Pork is eaten, according to some folklorists, because pigs do not "scratch" the earth the way chickens do and anyone who eats pork on New Year's Day will not have to scratch for a living in the coming year."

"You want to get off to a good start," said Frances Cattermole-Tally, executive editor of the Encyclopedia of American Popular Belief and Superstition, the first volume of which is to be published early next year by the University of California Press.

According to the volume, Ameri-

cans welcome the New Year with a wide panoply of good luck foods, including cabbage, herring, honey, sardines and salt.

The truth is that many of these culinary traditions are rooted in a simplistic rationale and the primitive notion that by putting a concept symbolically in one's mouth, one literally can embody it.

"You eat it; you swallow it; it becomes part of yourself," explained Barbara Kirshenblatt-Gimblett, an anthropologist and folklorist who is chairman of the Department of Performance Studies at New York University.
15   The symbols, too, are simplistic and their aspirations downright self-centered. Rather than addressing larger societal concerns like world peace and the benefit of mankind, they revolve around selfish wishes like personal gain, abundance, fertility and health.

Cattermole-Tally says, for example, that many Americans eat herring for the New Year because herring swim in such large numbers that they are a symbol of abundance. Eat a herring, the logic goes, and abundance will be yours in the new year.

In fact, fish are a favorite New Year's fare, Cattermole-Tally said because they swim forward and the belief is that people who eat fish will get ahead in the new year, too.

"So far it's worked for me," said Martha Henning, 77, a retired secretary in Washington Township, New Jersey, who has been eating herring every New Year's Eve since she was a young bride in 1934. "I've had a pretty lucky life."

William H. Wiggins, a professor of African American studies at Indiana University who is the author of "Oh Freedom!: Afro-American Emancipation Celebrations," (University of Tennessee) says that collard greens and cabbage are good luck foods because they are green and resemble money.

20 The quest for money in the new year is also seen in Italian customs. If Italians are not eating lentils, says Carol Field, author of "Celebrating Italy" (William Morrow), they are eating *chiacchiere*, pieces of dough that look like lentils and are drizzled with honey, so that the New Year will not only be prosperous but sweet.

In Piedmont, luck finds its vessel in risotto topped with melted fontina because it is a symbol of fertility.

"If you're really lucky, you get shavings of white truffles," Field points out.

In Rome, friends exchange dried figs soaked in honey. In southern Italy they prepare a lusty Sicilian creation that is a lasagna packed with ricotta cheese and topped with a dark tomato ragu.

Puns play an important role in the good luck foods of China and Japan. In Chinese, for example, the word *yu* means fish. Its homonym means surplus and abundance. Fish is therefore the omen of choice for the new year, which starts on Feb. 15, according to Charlie Chin, community education director of the New York Chinatown History Project.

25 Similarly, in Japan, according to Elizabeth Andoh, author of "An Ocean of Flavor: The Japanese Way with Fish and Seafood," (William Morrow), black beans are a food for the new year because they symbolize hard work and diligence.

Another popular New Year's custom in Japan, where at the stroke of midnight the temple bells ring 108 times to rid the world of evil, is eating *toshi koshi soba*, or year-end noodles.

These extremely long noodles are sucked into the mouth. They should not be cut on the theory that the longer the noodles, the longer and better the New Year.

In Ireland, the Celtic new year, traditionally Nov. 1, is often celebrated with a cake known as *barn brack*. It is filled with little symbols, each said to dictate one's fortune for the coming year. Guests do not know which of the charms they might receive.

A ring, for example, might indicate an impending marriage. A button, bachelorhood. A rag might predict poverty; a thimble, spinsterhood; a coin, wealth.

30 "In Ireland it's not so much good luck as what kind of luck might be out there," said Malachy McCormick, author of "Irish Country Cooking," (Clarkson Potter). He said his mother always prepared such a cake in his youth.

In India, the New Year celebrations at the end of October, the first and the middle of January focus on no one food but rather a balance of flavors, according to Julie Sahni, author of "Classic Indian Cooking," (Morrow).

Appam, a traditional cake made with rice flour, coconut, milk, and a kind of palm sap, is served along with a fudge called *barfi*. Both symbolize the wish for life to be sweet. But Sahni said other dishes, like mulligatawny soup (said to be good for a hangover) and green mango chutney, which is both sweet and hot, are served as well because a New Year's feast must include tastes that are at once sweet, savory, sour and hot.

"The idea is to serve something that brings many flavors in your mouth, with the hope that life is going to bring many elements of pleasure and pain and you should take it all in good spirit," Sahni said.

I. Getting the Message

A. After reading the article, choose the best answer for each item.

1. This article is mostly about
    a. how people celebrate the new year
    b. what people eat on New Year's and why
    c. whether a new year can bring good luck

2. One common belief is that eating fish will help a person be successful in life because
    a. fish live in water
    b. fish swim forward
    c. people everywhere eat fish

3. This article mostly describes
    a. scientific facts
    b. the author's personal beliefs
    c. traditional superstitions of various cultures

4. The information in this article is arranged mostly by
   a. nationality
   b. type of food
   c. religion

Check your answers with the key on page 169. If you have made mistakes, reread the article to gain a better understanding of it.

B. Reread "Food for Luck" for the information to complete the chart.

Food	Where Eaten	Why the Food Is Eaten for the New Year
long noodles		
pork		
black beans		
green cabbage		

II. Expanding Your Vocabulary

Getting Meaning from Context

Use context clues to find the meaning of each word, found in the paragraph indicated in parentheses. Choose the correct definition.

1. theorize (4):   a. offer as an explanation   b. refuse to accept as true
2. concoction (4):   a. a mixture   b. a drink
3. talismans (7):   a. tall men   b. things that have magical powers
4. superstition (11):   a. a traditional belief with no scientific basis   b. an important scientific theory
5. culinary (13):   a. related to ancient times   b. related to food
6. quest (20):   a. a search   b. a question
7. omen (24):   a. an indication of future events   b. a pun
8. impending (29):   a. having just happened recently   b. going to happen soon

III. Working with Idioms

Study the meanings of these idioms and expressions.

a dish (3, 4) = a particular combination of ingredients made into one recipe

scratch for a living (10) = work very hard for the money needed to live on

get off to a good start (11) = begin well

get ahead (17) = be successful

it's worked (18) = it has been successful

Complete these sentences, using the idioms and expressions.

1. People eat "lucky" foods for the New Year because they want the new year
to _____ for them.

2. According to one belief, people who eat pork on the New Year will have money and prosperity, and they will not have to _____.

3. Most New Year symbols do not center on the good of society; instead, they center on the individual's desire to _____ and make personal gains.

4. One woman, who says she has had a happy life, eats fish for the New Year, and she claims that _____ for her.

5. In many countries, people eat a traditional _____ for luck at the New Year.

IV. Making Sense of Sentences

Appositives are phrases that identify or tell more about a noun. They are usually set off from the rest of the sentence by commas. Here are two appositives in the article.

Paragraph 31: according to Julie Sahni, <u>author of "Classic Indian Cooking,"</u> . . .

Paragraph 32: *Appam*, <u>a traditional cake with rice flour, coconut, milk, and a kind of palm sap</u>, . . .

Look back at the paragraphs and notice how each appositive gives more information about the noun that comes before it. Note how the author often uses appositives to describe the foods, whose names probably will be unfamiliar to you.

Complete the following sentences by adding appositives. Use information from the indicated paragraph in the article to describe each food.

1. Vasilopita, _____, is eaten in Greece for the New Year. (paragraph 5).

2. Herring, _____, are eaten in America for a New Year of abundance. (paragraph 16)

3. In the southern United States, some people eat Hoppin' John, _____. (paragraph 3)

V. Talking and Writing

Discuss the following questions. Then choose one of them to write about.

1. Have you ever consulted a fortune-teller for advice or clues about your future? Did you follow the advice? Did the predictions come true?

2. Tell about a time when you had either good or bad luck.

3. People sometimes make resolutions at the start of a new year. They may promise to go on a diet or exercise more. What do you think of this practice of making resolutions? Have you ever made a resolution?

Arts and Leisure

Hey, Give Yourself a Break and Go Jump in a Hole

Previewing the Article

In a humorous way, the following article tells about the development of new recreational facilities in Tokyo, Japan. One of these is an unusual form of sky diving, a sport that usually involves jumping out of an airplane while wearing a parachute. Notice that the article is "framed" by an anecdote about sky diving in Tokyo. The author's personal experience begins and ends the article.

The title is both amusing and confusing because of its multiple meanings. What is the author suggesting by "Give yourself a break"? Literally, that could mean a broken bone. Idiomatically, it could mean two things: either a rest from work or an opportunity. Perhaps in the title it means all three. "Go jump in a hole" could be a rude way of saying "Go away," but, in this context, it is advice. However, after you finish the article, you may decide not to take that advice.

Before You Read

Before you read the article, discuss these questions.
1. Have you ever jumped out of an airplane? If so, describe the experience. If not, would you want to try it?
2. Worldwide, what is the reputation of Japanese workers?
3. Have you ever been in Tokyo? What do you know about the city?

As You Read

As you read, try to find out why Tokyo has so many new indoor recreational facilities.

Hey, Give Yourself a Break and Go Jump in a Hole

By T. R. Reid
The Washington Post

TOKYO—My knees are shaking, my heart is quaking and my head is encased in a crash helmet that seems much too thin. Perched at the edge of a narrow white platform, I am about to plunge headlong into a hot new phase of Japan's leisure craze: indoor sky diving, without a parachute.

I am deep into second thoughts, but there is no backing out now. To get out, I would have to climb back down the narrow ladder from the tower and walk past the long row of "salarymen" and "office ladies" lined up behind me at an amusement park named Tokyo Roof.

Tokyo Roof is one of hundreds of amusement parks, sports centers, resorts and arcades opening all over Japan as this hardworking nation brings its characteristic efficiency and intensity to the newly serious business of play.

There is a leisure boom in Japan, and like many national fads here it is largely a government-orchestrated phenomenon. Under pressure from the United States and other trading partners, who complain about workaholism in the labor force, Japan is working hard at the notion of working less hard.

5   Japanese workers labor about 200 more hours per year than the average of their American counterparts, according to Japan's Labor Ministry. With school in session every weekday plus Saturday morning 10 months of the year, Japanese students have almost 60 more class days annually than their American peers.

But now government and big business are vigorously promoting the concept of "leisure." Some companies require employees to take longer vacations, and others are moving to eliminate the traditional Saturday workday so that people will get out and recreate.

There is a problem for potential recreators in a tightly packed country where land is dear: There aren't many places to play. Designing cities in accordance with the Confucian dictum that hard work is a moral duty, those who rebuilt Japan after World War II left almost no room for recreation. Today, according to the Ministry of Construction, Tokyo has about 2.5 square meters of park for each resident.

To make up for the lack of public parkland, the private sector is devising all sorts of new entries in the leisure market. They include: indoor ski resorts, with mountains made of crushed ice inside airplane-hangar-sized buildings complete with chair lifts and ski schools; indoor mountain-climbing centers, with artificial peaks and cliffs; all-night golf courses, with floodlit fairways, fluorescent balls and blinking red lights atop the flag stick; golf driving ranges layered four stories high in the heart of the city, with towering green nets to keep the balls from smashing windows in neighboring office buildings.

Scores of amusement parks have opened since Tokyo Disneyland arrived in 1983, and 200 more are proposed or under construction. There is Sesame Land, complete with Bert, Ernie and Oscar; Pure Land; Aqua Adventure Land; Space World, and so forth. It is considered good form to give an amusement park a name in English, or at least quasi English. That explains the development of parks like Fruits Republic and Amazing Square.

10   Catering not only to children but also to young working singles, many amusement parks are pushing thrills. The Tokyo attraction called, inevitably, Coaster Land, has six roller coasters, including a sickening little number where the car spins 360 degrees, like a rolling pin, while whipping around the track.

And then there is Tokyo Roof, where I went sky diving indoors.

Set up on a downtown parking lot, its entrance marked by a massive sign that reads, in English, "Good Music from your Body heart on The World Line," Tokyo Roof is a test market for new amusement park ideas. It offers video-simulated golf courses, a race track where customers can drive scale Indianapolis-type cars, a movie theater where the seats roll and shake in accord with happenings on the screen. But its most popular attraction is the tall screened tower where I lined up.

For a fee of $15.60 per jump, Tokyo Roof rented me a flight suit, special shoes, gloves, earplugs, a motorcycle-style helmet, a face mask, a tooth guard and a safety harness (but no parachute).

Enswathed in this outfit, I waited in line for an hour with other adventurers, mostly office workers in their 20s. Finally it was my turn to climb the stairway and step out onto the narrow ledge.

15   I was looking into a 6-meter-high-cylinder of netting with a wire mesh floor. Taking directions from my "coach," who was standing at the bottom of the tower, I tightened my helmet, closed my eyes and leaped into the abyss.

I found myself suspended in mid-air—held aloft by a 130-kilometer-an-hour blast of wind coming from an industrial-strength fan in the bottom of the tower. This is the gimmick that permits indoor, parachute-free "sky diving." To my unspeakable relief, it worked.

For three minutes I flapped on the throbbing, pummeling, deafening funnel of wind. It did seem like sky diving, except that there is no diving involved; I floated at about the same level in the tower for the whole bone-shaking ride.

There was a trapeze bar hanging from the top of the tower, and I clutched at it for balance. I struggled futilely to respond to the instructions of my coach, who was shouting above the roar of the fan to tell me how to ride the wind funnel up and down, left and right, by bending various limbs.

Eventually I acquired just enough control to maneuver over to the exit platform. With my blood pressure going crazy but my pride intact, I stumbled out of the tower, only slightly shaken after a memorable bout with the Japanese concept of leisure.

I. Getting the Message

A. After reading the article, choose the best answer for each item.

1. This article is mainly about
   a. sky diving
   b. new recreational activities in Japan
   c. the author's fear of heights

2. The author found the Japanese version of sky diving
   a. boring
   b. scary
   c. similar to sky diving elsewhere

3. The author is writing about the new forms of recreation in Tokyo because he
   a. thinks the development is interesting and funny
   b. is worried that people may be injured doing these sports
   c. is upset that the Japanese are copying American ideas

4. Many new recreational facilities have been built in Tokyo recently because
   a. there was a lot of empty outdoor space to fill up
   b. the Japanese government didn't want its people to work so hard
   c. the Japanese people demanded more amusement facilities

5. Sky diving at the Tokyo Roof is different from the way the sport is enjoyed elsewhere because
   a. sky divers use a parachute
   b. it is an outdoor sport
   c. divers float on air currents made by a fan

6. One item that is *not* part of the equipment used in indoor sky diving is
   a. a flight suit
   b. earplugs
   c. a parachute

7. At the end of the article, the author
   a. feels relaxed after the sky dive
   b. requires the help of his coach to complete the dive
   c. is very relieved to have completed the dive

Check your answers with the key on page 169. If you have made mistakes, reread the article to gain a better understanding of it.

B. List three things mentioned in the article that show there is a trend toward more leisure in Japan.

II. Expanding Your Vocabulary

A. Getting Meaning from Context

Use context clues to determine the meaning of each word, found in the
paragraph indicated in parentheses. Choose the correct definition.

1. hot (1):   a. relating to warm weather   b. very popular activity
2. boom (4):   a. a loud noise   b. a sudden big growth or increase
3. peers (5):   a. teachers   b. people in the same situation
4. thrills (10):   a. rapidly moving cars   b. exciting activities
5. enswathed (14):   a. wrapped or dressed in   b. carrying in one's hand
6. abyss (15):   a. a deep empty space   b. a net
7. gimmick (16):   a. a clever method or device   b. a parachute
8. futilely (18):   a. successfully   b. without success

B. Reading for Suggested Meanings

Answer these questions.

1. In paragraph 1, the author is *perched* on a platform, waiting to sky-dive. Why is the word *perched* especially appropriate for sky diving?

2. In paragraph 4, the word *workaholism* is used. It has a negative meaning because it calls to mind alcoholism. What's the difference between a workaholic and a hardworking person?

3. In paragraph 9, does *quasi English* mean correct, formal English or similar to English?

4. In paragraph 19, the author says that his pride is still *intact*. Why?

5. In paragraph 19, the author talks about having a *bout* with the Japanese concept of leisure. The word *bout* can mean an athletic match, such as a boxing match. Does the use of the word suggest that the author found the experience relaxing?

III. Working with Idioms

Study the meanings of these idioms and expressions.

From the headline:

hey = exclamation used to get a person's attention

a break = a rest from work, an opportunity

go jump in a hole = go away, and stop bothering me. (*Go jump into a lake* is a variation of this expression.)

From the article:

deep in . . . thought (2) = thinking hard, not paying attention to what is happening around you

second thoughts (2) = reconsidering a past decision

back out (2) = not do something you had agreed to do

push (an idea or activity) (10) = encourage people to do it

go crazy (19) = show a very high level of enthusiasm or activity, be out of control

Answer these questions.

1. In paragraph 2, what is the author having *second thoughts* about?
2. In paragraph 2, why does the author want to *back out* of jumping?
3. In paragraph 10, what are examples of activities that amusement parks are *pushing*?
4. In paragraph 19, why is the author's blood pressure *going crazy*?

 ## IV. Focusing on Style and Tone

This article is funny because of the contradictory things that the author describes: for example, *indoor sky diving* and *required vacations*. The author also expresses ideas in ways that emphasize contradiction: for example, *working hard at the notion of working less hard* or *I waited in line with other adventurers, mostly office workers.* Reread paragraph 8, and find two other examples of contradictions. List them.

 ## V. Talking and Writing

Discuss the following topics. Then choose one of them to write about.

1. Have you ever done anything dangerous? Did you enjoy it?
2. There are two main types of leisure-time activities. One is entertainment (a passive experience, such as watching TV or watching a ball game). The other is recreation (doing something for fun and relaxation). Which is better for people? Do people need both? Do some people overdo one or the other?
3. What is your favorite leisure-time activity, and how has it enriched your life?
4. What's wrong with being a workaholic? In your opinion, who suffers most—the workaholic person, co-workers or family members?

Arts and Leisure

Art, Photography, Copyright and the Law

Previewing the Article

Look at the photographs accompanying this article. Two happy people and their "string of puppies" became the subject of an important legal controversy. The argument occurred between two artists who preserved this scene in different media.

The photograph on the left was taken by professional photographer Art Rogers. An artist named Jeff Koons made four sculptures that closely resembled Rogers's photograph. (The picture on the right shows one of the four Koons sculptures.) Koons sold three of them for $367,000. Did Koons have the right to use Rogers's photograph without permission or payment? Rogers's photograph was copyrighted. That gave him the right to prevent others from copying his work.

But Koons argued that the First Amendment to the U.S. Constitution, which guarantees free speech and expression, gave him the right to express his ideas. He claimed that he had an original idea—the idea of making a sculpture out of Rogers's photograph—and that the copyright laws could not prevent him from expressing his idea.

The newspaper article was written before the U.S. Court of Appeals heard the case, so you can read the arguments on both sides and judge for yourself. If you are interested in who won the appeal from the Court of Appeals, look at the box on page 113.

Before You Read

Before you read the article, discuss these questions.

1. Look at the two pictures carefully. What similarities and differences do you notice?

2. What is a copyright, and what is copyright infringement? (Use a dictionary for help, if necessary.)

3. In the U.S. Constitution, what rights does the First Amendment guarantee?

4. Have you ever been involved in a lawsuit? What was the case about? Was it appealed to a higher court?

As You Read

As you read, look for arguments that support each artist's position.

Art, Photography, Copyright and the Law

By Constance L. Hays
New York Times Service

NEW YORK—Three years ago, the artist Jeff Koons, who had decided to create a sculpture called "String of Puppies," sent a greeting card that he had bought in an airport gift shop to his workers in Italy, telling them that the sculpture "must be just like photo" on the card.

The photograph, which featured a couple holding eight German shepherd puppies, became the model for four Koons sculptures, three of which sold for a total of $367,000 after being shown at the Sonnabend Gallery in Manhattan.

Koons's supporters applauded. Art Rogers sued.

It was Rogers's photograph that Koons used—without permission—in what Rogers called an infringement on his copyright.

5 Now, the art world and copyright lawyers are watching an appeal of Rogers's original lawsuit, which they say raises some critical questions: What is art? At what point does artistic freedom end and copyright infringement begin? And will enforcing copyright restrictions deprive artists of their First Amendment rights?

In some ways, they say, the court is being asked to help determine the legitimacy of a fairly recent genre in which items from popular culture are borrowed and sometimes reshaped to make social criticisms.

"This is a difficult case because there are First Amendment issues on both sides," said Kathleen M. Sullivan, a Harvard law School professor who has testified in similar art cases. "Will the Rogerses of the world be intimidated if they're not protected from theft, or will the Koonses of the world be stymied because their sources are cut off? It's a toss-up."

Last December, a federal judge in Manhattan agreed with Rogers, who is a photographer in California. The judge ruled that Koons, who faces similar charges in three other lawsuits, had used Rogers's work in a way that violated copyright laws.

But because Rogers and Koons sought a ruling but not a trial, the judge said he could not decide if Rogers should receive damages, namely part of the $367,000 paid for the three sold statues.

10 Neither side was happy and both appealed the lower court ruling. The

NYT PICTURES

Photograph of eight German Shepherd puppies by Art Rogers

NYT PICTURES

Jeff Koons's sculpture "String of Puppies." Is it a true artistic expression or an attempt to make money?

appeal is to be heard next month in the U.S. Court of Appeals for the 2d Circuit in Manhattan.

"The lower court simply did not understand the social critique that is embedded in this artistic tradition," said Michael D. Rips, one of the lawyers representing Koons.

"Basically, these artists see society as overrun by consumerism. They pull items out of mass culture and comment critically on those items. It's not something judges are terribly familiar with, and part of the process in Koons's case is educating the judges."

To Koons, his lawyers said, the photograph of the couple and puppies was part of the wide trough of American popular culture from which he draws inspiration. Rogers's photography simply happened to be the image that he chose for his sculpture, his lawyers said, after more than two years of collecting similar images in notebooks.

Rogers disagrees, of course. He said he felt "totally ripped off" after seeing a photograph of Koons's work, which had many similarities to his own.

15 "This is elevating stealing to some level of art," said Rogers, who produces a weekly photo column called the Point Reyes Family Album for a newspaper in Point Reyes, California.

"Nothing is sacred to Koons. No one has any privacy, any rights, because he is parodying it as a great artist who can do this in the name of art. Can he kill somebody in the name of art? Where do you draw the line?"

In his lawsuit, Rogers accused Koons of "reappropriation," saying that although the photograph of the puppies was public, it had been copyrighted and was protected against unauthorized use.

Just how much Koons transformed the photograph is part of the debate. Koons's lawyers contend that by creating a sculpture, Koons developed a whole new form.

They added that the addition of colors and other details—like daisies sprouting from the people's hair and ears, and a bright blue cast on the puppies—distinguished his sculptures even further from the photograph. At the same time, they say, using Italian artisans who normally carve crucifixes and church sculptures elevated the image to beatific heights, "like a Pietà."

20 Moreover, Jeff Koons and his lawyers say, even if Rogers wanted to create his own sculpture based on "Puppies," there would be no loss to him because it would be an Art Rogers, not a Jeff Koons.

Others are less convinced. "Basically, he has appropriated somebody else's work for his own use," said Stephen E. Weil, an author of books on art law and a deputy director of the Hirschhorn Museum and Sculpture Garden in Washington.

"It would be preposterous to think that you could write a novel, and then somebody else could come along and break it up into a lot of short stories and say it's a totally different thing."

Much of the controversy seems to stem from disagreement about Koons's art. His supporters depict him as a wunderkind whose stark postmodernism descends from the best in American and European art. His critics call him market-driven, among other things.

Koons, a former Wall Street trader, made a name for himself in the 1980s by encasing vacuum cleaners in Plexiglas boxes and casting stainless-steel replicas of inflatable rabbits.

25 Such a tradition can be linked to artists like Marcel Duchamp, his lawyers argue, who set the Paris art world on its ear at the turn of the century by placing a urinal in a major exhibition.

There are also ties to Andy Warhol, they say, who transformed a modest can of soup into something to grace the living room walls.

"Since 1979, Koons has been making art that provokes thought," wrote I. Michael Danoff in a catalog for a Koons show at the Museum of Contemporary Art in Chicago. "Koons communicates through a heightened sense of symbolism. He attaches a profusion of meaning to the things he sees and likewise to those objects he presents as art."

Yve-Alain Bois, a professor of modern art at Harvard University, disagrees. "As far as my own judgment," he said, "his work is totally trivial and a pure product of the market. He's considered to be an heir to Duchamp, but I think it's a trivialization of all that. I think he's kind of a commercial artist."

Amid so many flaring opinions, the case of Art Rogers vs. Jeff Koons and Sonnabend Gallery will try for a resolution in the appeals court. Meanwhile, the fourth version of "String of Puppies" languishes in a warehouse, under court order.

I. Getting the Message

A. After reading the article, indicate if each statement is true (*T*) or false (*F*).

_____ 1. Most legal experts agree that the law clearly supports Koons.

_____ 2. Rogers received a large sum of money as a result of the judge's decision.

_____ 3. According to Koons's lawyers, Koons's purpose in using Rogers's photograph was to criticize mass culture.

_____ 4. Art experts do not agree on the artistic value of Koons's work.

Check your answers with the key on page 170. If you have made mistakes, reread the article to gain a better understanding of it.

B. Do these statements help Koons's case, do they help Rogers's case or are they unrelated to the controversy?
Identify each statement by making a check (✔) in the correct box.

K = pro-Koons, the sculptor
R = pro-Rogers, the photographer
I = irrelevant (not supporting either side)

	K	R	I
1. Koons told his workers to make the sculptures look exactly the same as the photograph.			
2. Many artists have used items from popular culture in their works.			
3. The Koons sculptures are not exactly the same as the Rogers photograph.			
4. The Rogers photograph was copyrighted.			
5. Photography and sculpture are very different art forms.			
6. Koons is a famous artist, and Rogers is not.			
7. An artist's creative work is his or her property, and no one has the right to steal it.			
8. Some people think that Koons is more interested in making money than in making art.			

II. Expanding Your Vocabulary

A. Getting Meaning from Context

Use context clues to determine the meaning of each word, found in the paragraph indicated in parentheses. Choose the correct definition.

1. deprive (5):
   a. protect
   b. take away or remove

2. genre (6):
   a. a type of artistic work
   b. postmodern art

3. issues (7):
   a. matters in dispute because people have different opinions about them
   b. particular copies of a magazine, journal or newspaper

4. stymied (7):
   a. prevented from acting
   b. assisted

5. charges (8):
   a. costs
   b. accusations of wrongdoing

6. damages (9):
   a. injuries
   b. payment for injuries

7. contend (18):
   a. say, claim
   b. be satisfied

8. preposterous (22):
   a. ridiculous
   b. logical

9. provokes (27):
   a. annoys, angers
   b. arouses, causes

10. resolution (29):
    a. final decision
    b. strong will to do something

B. Finding Words That Don't Belong

In this list of 15 words from the article, nine have a meaning related to the law, and six do not. Indicate the ones that are related to the law.

appeal	damages	testified
case	market	trial
charges	profusion	transform
consumer	replica	vacuum
court	sue	vs. (versus)

III. Working with Idioms

Study the meanings of these idioms and expressions.

cut off (7) = end a connection, stop

toss-up (7) = even chance, 50-50 chance (such as the chance of a tossed coin landing heads or tails)

ripped off (14) = cheated, robbed

Nothing is sacred to . . . (16) = The person doesn't respect anything

in the name of (16) = for the sake of, in support of

draw the line (16) = set the limit

market-driven (23) = primarily concerned with selling things

wunderkind (23) = wonder child, an unusually talented or intelligent child

make a name for oneself (24) = become famous

set . . . on its ear (25) = surprise and upset it

Complete the sentences, using the idioms and expressions. Use the correct verb tense.

1. Jeff Koons was called a _____ because he became famous when he was young.

2. He _____ as an artist whose work parodied popular culture.

3. It's O.K. for one artist to be influenced by the work of another, but artists shouldn't steal from one another. No one should be _____.

4. Artists can't commit crimes _____ art. We have to _____ somewhere.

5. Rogers said that Koons had no respect for anyone or anything. "_____," Rogers said.

IV. Making Sense of Sentences

The word *who* is often used as a relative pronoun at the beginning of an adjective clause. *Who* always refers to a person or to people, never to a thing. There are two types of adjective clauses.

Type 1: Restrictive clauses
These are needed to identify the noun they modify.

Rogers was the photographer *who sued Koons.*
(*The adjective clause identifies the specific photographer.*)

Type 2: Nonrestrictive clauses
These describe the noun they modify, but they aren't necessary to identify the noun. In the following example, the person is already identified by his name, so the adjective clause is merely descriptive, providing additional information. Nonrestrictive clauses are often set off from the rest of the sentence with commas.

The lawsuit was started by Art Rogers, *who hoped to receive damages.*

Complete the chart by writing the adjective clause beginning with *who,* the person (or people) that the clause modifies and then the type of clause (1 or 2).

Paragraph	Adjective Clause	Whom Does It Describe?	Type
1	who had decided to create a sculpture called "String of Puppies"	Jeff Koons	2
8			
15			
16			
19			
25			

V. Talking and Writing

A. Argue the appeal of the Koons-Rogers case. The lawyers for each side should state their arguments in class. Then, as a class, vote to decide who won the appeal.

B. Discuss the following topics. Then choose one of them to write about.

1. Do you think Koons changed Rogers's photograph enough to make it his own creation? If not, how much change would be enough? Where do you draw the line between being inspired by someone else's work and copying it?

2. Disputes between two Americans often end up in court. If you were Art Rogers, would you have handled the matter another way? If so, what would you have done differently?

3. Were you more sympathetic toward Rogers or Koons? What information affected your attitude?

Who won the appeal?
Rogers the photographer won it.

Arts and Leisure

Is There a European Accent in Euro Disneyland?

Previewing the Articles

Mickey Mouse learned to say "bienvenue" before he came to France, but that didn't guarantee that the French would welcome him. Before the grand opening of Euro Disneyland outside of Paris, people everywhere were wondering if Europeans would like this hectic, exciting, crowded, expensive form of American recreation. Would Europeans bring their kids and leave their money, or would Euro Disney be rejected as a "cultural Chernobyl"? Would Euro Disney be the site of a pleasant blend of cultures or a painful clash? Would it make money and expand, or lose money and close?

The first article in this chapter was printed a few months before opening day of the park. It explains why Euro Disney might succeed or fail. The follow-up article, printed a few months after the opening, provides short-term answers to some of the questions raised in the first. Did Euro Disney do better or worse than expected? Did the French and other Europeans support it? The article, which focuses on finances, also raises new questions. No doubt, the story of Euro Disney will be continued in future articles.

Before You Read

Before you read the two articles, discuss these questions.
1. What is a theme park? Have you ever visited one? What was its theme? What did you see and do there? Why do you think theme parks are popular?
2. Have you ever been to a Disney theme park? What are its major themes? Did you enjoy the attractions?

As You Read

As you read the first article, look for advantages and possible problems that the Disney organization faces in its new location.

Is There a European Accent in Euro Disneyland?

By Barry James
International Herald Tribune

PARIS—Does Mickey Mouse have whiskers?

No.

Does this mean that Frenchmen seeking work with the Disney organization must shave off their mustaches too?

It depends.

5   A labor inspector took the Disney organization to court this week, contending that the company's squeaky clean dress and appearance code—which bans mustaches, beards, excess weight, short skirts and fancy hose—offends individual liberty and contravenes French labor law.

The case is an illustration of some of the tricky cultural issues the company faces as it gets ready to open its theme park in Marne-la-Vallée, 20 miles (32 kilometers) east of Paris in five months' time.

The Disney management, which is assembling what it calls a "cast" of 12,000 to run the theme park, argues that all employees, from bottle washers to the president, are akin to actors who have to obey rules about appearance. Anyway, a company spokesman says, no one has yet put his mustache before a job. As one new "cast member" put it: "You must believe in what you are doing, or you would have a terrible time here."

For all its concern about foreign cultural invasion and its rearguard defense against the spread of franglais, France's Socialist government has been complacent about the implantation of such a huge American icon on the doorstep of the capital. It made an extraordinary series of tax and financial concessions to attract the theme park here rather than let it go to sunnier Spain. Disney struck a deal of which Uncle Scrooge could have been proud. It took title to a 1,940-hectare (4,800-acre) expanse of land one fifth the size of Paris.

Toon Town itself will be only part of a giant complex of housing, office and resort developments stretching far into the next century, including movie and television production facilities. As part of its deal with the Disney organization, the government is laying on and paying for new highways, an extension of Paris's RER regional express railway and even a direct connection for the high speed TGV railway to the Channel Tunnel. The TGV station is being built in front of the main entrance of Euro Disneyland, and is scheduled to come into service in 1994.

10 If Euro Disneyland succeeds—where theme parks already in France have so far failed—a second and even a third park is likely to be built by the end of the century. Financial analysts say that Euro Disneyland, the first phase of which is costing an estimated $3.6 billion, is essential to Disney's overall fortunes, which have been hit by competition and declining attendance in the United States.

French intellectuals have not found many kind things to say about the project. In a celebrated comment, Marguerite Duras likened it to a "cultural Chernobyl." The kids, however, will probably never notice. Sleeping Beauty, Snow White, Peter Pan, Alice in Wonderland or Pinocchio all come from European fairy tales or stories and are as familiar to children here as they are in the United States. To a French child Mickey is French. To an Italian kid he is Topolino—and Italian.

The Disney management is stressing this heritage in an apparent response to suggestions that it is culturally imperialistic. Although the conception of the theme park is closely based on the original Magic Kingdom in California and the Walt Disney World in Florida, "Euro Disneyland will be unique in a manner befitting its European home," the company says. "The legends and fairy tales which originated in Europe figure prominently in the creative development of the theme park." Officials point out,

for example, that Sleeping Beauty's turreted castle in Fantasyland, the central feature of the theme park, is based not on Hollywood, as some might think, but on the illustrations in a medieval book of hours, "Les Très Riches Heures du Duc de Berry."

The company experimented with 27 different kinds of paint, however, before it came up with the exact hue to make the castle look Florida pink even when it is raining in Paris.

The olde worlde fairground horses on "Lancelot's carousel" were carved by hand after what Disney calls "a quest for that elusive artisan: the old-time craftsman." Geppetto? No. The artisans were found in the United States.

15 The 360-degree movie that will be showed in the "visionarium," based on the adventures of Jules Verne, features well-known European actors such as Michel Piccoli, Gérard Depardieu and Nathalie Baye.

Asked to describe other aspects of Europeanization, a spokesman mentioned that direction signs in the theme park will be in French as well as English, and that buccaneers in the pirate's lair will banter in French, Spanish and English. "The challenge is telling things people already know—and at the same time making it different," the spokesman said.

On the other hand, Europeanization is not being taken too far. Nicholas de Schonen, another Disney spokesman, said earlier that the aim of the theme park is to provide a basically American experience for those who seek it. In this way, he said, people

who might otherwise have contemplated a vacation in the United States will be happy to stay on this side of the Atlantic.

To this end, the company is building a resort area with "themed" hotels—turn-of-the-century gothic and New York-style opulence for the well-heeled; the Newport Bay Club and Sequoia for the less affluent; the Hotel Cheyenne and Hotel Sante Fe for those of "moderate" means and Camp Davy Crockett for the hoi polloi.

The Disney organization does seem to have a bit of an obsession about hirsuteness. "Main Street, USA," the hub of Euro Disneyland, it promises, will feature an old time "Harmony Barber Shop" to deal with "scraggly hair and stubbly chins"—and perhaps even offending mustaches. One difference from California or Florida: Parts of Main Street and waiting areas to get into the attractions will be covered over as a concession to Paris's quirky weather.

20 Euro Disneyland's proximity to Paris is an undeniable attraction. Anyone tiring of Ameriana or ersatz European culture can reach the Louvre by express railway in less than an hour—from Minnie to Mona in a flash.

Communications figured large in the Disney organization's decision to site its fourth theme park near Paris. The site is within a two-hour flight of 320 million Europeans. The opening of Eastern Europe is another bonanza for the company, which thinks that millions of people will put Disneyland top of a list of places to visit on their first trip to the West.

I. Getting the Message: First Article

A. After reading the article, indicate if each item is true (*T*) or false (*F*).

_____ 1. The French government tried to prevent Euro Disney from coming to France.

_____ 2. The financial success of Euro Disney is important to the Walt Disney Company.

_____ 3. Disney has very strict rules about the way its employees look.

_____ 4. All male employees at Euro Disney are required to have mustaches so that they look French.

_____ 5. A visit to Euro Disney is primarily a European experience with a few American touches.

_____ 6. Euro Disney aims at attracting people of all economic means.

Check your answers with the key on page 170. If you have made mistakes,
reread the article to gain a better understanding of it.

B. The financial success of Euro Disney was uncertain when it opened.

1. Scan the article for reasons why Euro Disney might succeed. What are two of them?

2. Scan the article for reasons why Euro Disney might fail. What are two of them?

II. Expanding Your Vocabulary

A. Getting Meaning from Context

Use context clues to determine the meaning of each word, found in the
paragraph(s) indicated in parentheses. Choose the correct definition.

1. complacent (8):   a. angry   b. satisfied

2. icon (8):   a. a representation of some- b. an unpopular theme park
                            thing highly respected

3. concession (8, 19):   a. something given   b. something taken

4. figure (12, 21):   a. think out   b. be considered as part of a plan

5. hirsuteness (19):   a. noise   b. hairiness

6. quirky (19):   a. peculiar and likely to   b. pleasant and mild
                            change suddenly

7. proximity (20):   a. nearness   b. great distance

8. ersatz (20):   a. popular and familiar   b. a kind of substitute

9. bonanza (21):   a. a source of great and   b. a serious financial problem
                            sudden wealth or luck

B. Reading for Suggested Meanings

Choose the phrase that completes each sentence correctly.

1. According to paragraph 7, Disney management calls its employees a "cast." This suggests
   that they are all
   a. very similar in appearance
   b. playing a role in a theatrical production

2. In paragraph 11, Euro Disney is compared to a "cultural Chernobyl." The person quoted
   believes that Euro Disney will be
   a. a good influence on French culture
   b. a bad influence on French culture

3. According to paragraph 18, the *well-heeled* are
   a. richer than the hoi polloi
   b. poorer than the hoi polloi

4. In paragraph 19, the author says that Disney has "an obsession about hirsuteness." The
   word *obsession* suggests that the author
   a. agrees with Disney
   b. doesn't agree with Disney

III. Working with Idioms

Study the meanings of these idioms and expressions.

squeaky clean (5) = very clean

put something before something else (7) = give the first thing greater priority or importance

on the doorstep of (8) = near, just outside of

franglais (8) = French (français) with a lot of English (anglais) in it

strike a deal (8) = make a business agreement

hit by (10) = hurt by

to this end (18) = with this goal in mind, for this purpose

turn-of-the-century (18) = the end of one century and beginning of the next (usually, around 1900)

in a flash (20) = quickly

It's put top of the list. (21) = It will be done first.

Study the meanings and sources of these famous names.

Mickey and Minnie Mouse (1, 20) = Disney cartoon characters

Scrooge (8) = a very stingy character from Charles Dickens's short novel *A Christmas Carol*

Toon Town (9) = home of cartoon characters (In this article, it refers to the Euro Disney theme park area, not the resorts.)

Chernobyl (11) = a city in the Ukraine (the site of a nuclear plant disaster in 1986)

Geppetto (14) = the man who carved the puppet Pinocchio (in the famous Italian children's story)

Mona (Lisa) (20) = the woman in Leonardo Da Vinci's famous painting. (It hangs in the Louvre museum in Paris.)

Answer these questions.

1. Why wouldn't a stingy person want to stay at Euro Disney's opulent *turn-of-the-century* hotel?
2. Is Disneyland put *on the top of your list* of vacation spots? Why, or why not?
3. How can a tourist go from Minnie to Mona *in a flash*?
4. In paragraph 7, a Disney spokesman says, "... no one has yet put his mustache before a job." What does that mean?
5. According to paragraph 8, Euro Disney is *on the doorstep of* the capital. What does that mean?

Reading a Follow-up Article

Gloss Is Off at Euro Disney As Park Predicts a Loss

As You Read

As you read the second article about Euro Disney, look for the changes that the Disney organization is planning in order to make the park more profitable.

Gloss Is Off at Euro Disney As Park Predicts a Loss

By Roger Cohen
New York Times Service

PARIS—Euro Disney SCA, acknowledging that its elaborate theme park had not performed as strongly as expected, announced Thursday that it would incur a net loss of unpredictable magnitude in its first financial year.

At the time of the April opening of the park, which stands on a 1,900-hectare (4,800 acre) site 30 kilometers (20 miles) east of Paris, Euro Disney officials said they expected to make a small profit for the financial year ending Sept. 30. But since then the park has been hit by a number of problems.

"We were geared up for a very high level of operations," the company's chief financial officer, John Forsgren, said in a telephone interview. "It has been very strong, but not as strong as we geared up for.

"While attendance is very strong," he said, "our cost levels do require adjustment for the current revenue level."

5   In Burbank, California, Walt Disney Co. said Thursday that its earnings rose 33 percent in the quarter. But it warned investors against expecting profits soon from Euro Disney, of which it owns 49 percent.

Euro Disney said that although attendance levels had been high, "the company anticipates that it will incur a net loss for the fiscal year ending Sept. 30, 1992."

It added that "the magnitude of the loss will depend on attendance and hotel-occupancy rates achieved during the remainder of the critical European summer vacation period."

The announcement amounted to an extraordinary turnabout for Euro Disney, which opened amid immense fanfare and widespread predictions of immediate success.

At the time of the opening, on April 12, the company's shares were trading at 140.90 francs ($28.07), and had been as high as 170 francs earlier in the year. They dropped 2.75 percent Thursday to close at 97.25 francs.

10   Mr. Forsgren said he thought the market had "overreacted a bit emotionally to preliminary information." He added that "by all objective standards the park is very successful. The long-term acceptance is strong, the rest is just details."

The company said that 3.6 million people had visited the park from April 12 to July 22, a performance it said was superior to that of comparable start-up periods at other Disney theme parks. But it cautioned that, given the likely strong seasonal fluctuations in attendance, no inference about future attendance or profitability should be drawn.

Reacting to the announcement, Paribas Capital Markets Group issued a "sell" recommendation on Euro Disney stock, saying that attendance levels for the period were 15 percent below its expectations and spending on food and other merchandise was 10 percent below. It predicted that the company would lose 300 million francs in the current financial year and continue losing money for two more years.

The main problem confronting Euro Disney appears to be managing its costs and finding an appropriate price level for its over 5,000 hotel rooms. Clearly, costs have been geared to a revenue level that has not been achieved, and the company is beginning to drop hotel prices that have been widely described as exorbitant.

Mr. Forsgren said staffing, now at 17,000, would "come down signifi-cantly in the next two months, mainly through the attrition of seasonal employees." Of the current staff, 5,000 were employed on a temporary basis, he said.

15   He also acknowledged that the lowest-priced rooms at the resort had been cut to 550 francs ($110) from 750 francs at the time of the opening, and that some rooms were being offered at 400 francs for the winter season. Analysts believe hotel occupancy has been running at about 68 percent, although it is currently over 90 percent.

"The key issue is costs," said Paul Slattery, an analyst at Kleinwort Benson in London. "They have no idea what their winter attendance levels will be and they're battling to get costs to an appropriate level. The stock's still overpriced, but I think in the long term they'll get it right."

Still, huge uncertainty hangs over the company's plans to keep the theme park open through the cold European winter—something no other theme park in Europe has ever attempted.

Last month, the company said it was having difficulty attracting people from the Paris region. Mr. Forsgren said that French attendance was improving and accounted for 1 million of the 3.6 million visitors, with most of the rest coming from Britain and Germany. Only 1 percent of visitors have been American.

For its third quarter ended June 30, the first in which the park has been operating, the company announced revenues of 2.47 billion francs ($492 million), but gave no profit or loss figures in line with French practice for quarterly results. In the first half, the company earned 75 million francs, mainly from financial income and sale of construction rights on its site.

IV. Getting the Message: Follow-up Article

After reading the follow-up article, put a check (✔) in the correct column
to indicate increases and decreases at Euro Disney.

	Going Up	Going Down	Not Discussed
1. number of employees			
2. prices of hotel rooms			
3. amount of advertising			
4. French attendance			
5. price of admission			
6. value of Euro Disney stock			

Check your answer with the key on page 170. If you have made mistakes,
reread the article to gain a better understanding of it.

V. Making Sense of Sentences

In the follow-up article, many sentences contain words that connect contrasting ideas. Study some of these sentences in paragraphs 2 and 3 (*but*),
paragraph 4 (*while*), paragraph 15 (*although*) and paragraph 17 (*still*).

Now write sentences using these four words to contrast the following ideas.
- Attendance at Euro Disney has been high.
- Euro Disney expects to lose money during its first year in operation.

1. *but* _____

2. *while* _____

3. *although* _____

4. *still* _____

VI. Talking and Writing

Discuss the following topics. Then choose one of them to write about.

1. If Disney wanted to open a theme park in your native country, do you think most people
    would welcome it or object to it? Do you think attendance would be high?

2. What influence has American culture had upon your native country? Do you think the influ-
    ence has been good or bad?

3. Do you think theme parks provide entertainment that is physically and mentally beneficial
    to people?

FOCUS ON THE NEWSPAPER

Arts and Leisure

Analyzing Reviews and Profiles

The newspaper provides information about goings-on in the world of art and entertainment. It is a handy, up-to-date, inexpensive source of information about ways to spend leisure time.

Newspapers provide information on arts and leisure in many kinds of feature articles. The focus here is on two of these article types: the review and the profile.

The Review

Newspapers often give readers opinions on various forms of entertainment. Readers want to know: should I see this play or movie, buy this book, or visit this museum? Is it worth my time and money? Will I enjoy it or learn from it? A good review does several things: it describes, analyzes and evaluates. Readers find out how a particular work compares to others of the same type. Readers also get an opinion regarding the strengths, weaknesses and overall quality of a work.

Exercise 1: Reviewing the Reviews

Look in the entertainment section of a newspaper. Select three reviews to read: they may be of a movie, book, play, concert, art exhibit or some other artistic work or form of entertainment. (Note: Some newspapers regularly have an entertainment section that contains reviews. In addition, once a week there may be a separate section with reviews of current entertainment or with reviews of books. These are good sources for you to refer to.) Read the reviews carefully. Then complete a chart like this.

Analyzing a Review				
Type/Name of Entertainment (Movie, Concert, etc.)	Brief Description	Strengths	Weaknesses	Author's Overall Evaluation

Exercise 2: Be the Reviewer

Prepare a short review of some leisure-time activity you have enjoyed (or not enjoyed) recently. Tell whether or not you recommend this particular activity and why.

The Profile

The public has a great deal of curiosity about celebrities in entertainment and the arts, such as movie stars, singers, writers, artists. Newspapers often run articles called *profiles*, which give readers a better understanding of artists and entertainers.

Profiles typically give the following kinds of information to readers:
- tell something about the celebrity's personal life
- tell about the celebrity's current work or production
- reveal the person's professional goals, style, sources of inspiration and attitudes toward his or her career

Information in a profile comes from the journalist's interview with a famous person. A profile usually contains many direct quotations, so that readers share the experience of actually hearing the subject of the profile talk.

A good profile makes readers feel that they know and understand the person being interviewed. Often, this leads to a better understanding and enjoyment of the person's work.

Exercise 3: What's in a Profile?

Find a profile in a newspaper. Analyze the profile by answering these questions.

Analyzing a Profile

1. Why did the newspaper run a profile on this person at this time? _____

2. Did you know anything about the person before you read the article? _____
   If so, did the article cause you to change your attitude toward this person? Did you find out anything new that surprised you about the person? _____

3. Did the article stimulate your interest in the person's work? Why, or why not? _____

4. How do you think the author of the profile felt toward the subject? _____
   What paragraph or words gave you the best clue? _____

   _____

5. What influenced your impression of the subject the most: the quotations from the person being profiled or the comments of the writer of the profile? _____

6. What would you like to know about the subject that the article did not tell you? _____

   _____

Science
& Environment

Science and Environment

Even the Palawan Stink Badger Has Its Defenders

Previewing the Article

Can you name the most dangerous animal on earth? It's the human being. Technology has made people too powerful for their own good. Fortunately, there are some people smart enough to know this. Many of them have organized into groups, and they work hard to prevent people from foolishly killing off other species.

But why should people spend money and effort to keep endangered species alive if the animals are dangerous or disgusting? The following article answers that question.

Before You Read

Before you read the article, do these activities:

1. Look for photographs of these animals: tiger, elephant, bat, rat, crocodile, condor, oryx and badger. You can find all of them in an encyclopedia.
2. Discuss these questions: Are there any animals you dislike? Do you think the world would be a better place without them?
3. Discuss reasons why some plants and animals are becoming extinct. How and why do modern civilization and human greed threaten some species?

As You Read

Look at the picture accompanying this article. The picture shows a clever trick used by people who work in wildlife reserves. A wildlife reserve is a place where animals can live in a protected environment. But the workers in one such reserve were in danger from the resident tigers. The workers solved the problem by becoming "two-faced." Read the article to find out about the nature of the trick.

Even the Palawan Stink Badger Has Its Defenders

By Barry James
International Herald Tribune

A two-faced approach is keeping tigers off people's backs in Bengal, and therein lies a tale about keeping rare species alive.

Noting that the fearsome Sunderban tiger in West Bengal attacks men only from behind, wildlife management authorities at the tiger reserves there send honey collectors and other workers into the mangrove forest with rubber masks tied to the backs of their heads.

Since that method was adopted in 1987, not a single worker wearing a mask has been attacked—but 30 workers who preferred to put their faith in traditional deities or who neglected to put on the masks were killed in one year, according to Peter Jackson, an expert on big cats.

The story is one of the successes in the mostly losing battle of ensuring the survival of wildlife species amid spreading civilization that both destroys their habitats and destroys them because of aversion, greed, neglect or fear.

5   This weekend, about 200 specialists belonging to the Species Survival Commission will meet in Rome to discuss how that battle should best be conducted.

They are to draw up a plan called "Heritage Species" to protect some of the world's more threatened plants and animals—which include the elephant, of course, but also less endearing beasties such as vampire bats, black rats, crocodiles, and Palawan stink badgers.

The idea of equipping human beings with rearward-facing masks—in effect, adopting the mimicry defense of many animal species—along with other methods such as sending workers into the forest dressed in suits of plastic armor and setting up electrified dummy humans, has helped reduce the casualty rate and thus lessen the fric-

Nicolae Asciu

tion between people and the Sunderban tiger.

This has made it possible to ensure the survival of the tigers, whose numbers have doubled under a program launched in 1973 with support from the World Wildlife Fund.

"The maintenance of biological diversity has got to be one of the highest environmental priorities in the world," said Mark Halle, director of field operations for the International Union for Conservation of Nature and Natural Resources in Gland, Switzerland. The organization, which groups governments, government agencies and nongovernment organizations such as the Sierra Club, is the parent of the Species Survival Commission.

10   Mr. Halle acknowledged that it was difficult to get people to dig into their pockets to save some of life's more unpleasant varmints.

"There are all sorts of species that we have a hard time finding arguments for," he said. "And one of the things that does environmentalists poor credit is to insist overly for any particular individual species. The millions that went into saving the California Condor, for example, as far as I'm concerned could have been better spent."

Nevertheless, Mr. Halle said, genetic diversity is important and man ought to think carefully about the wider consequences before allowing any species to die out.

Everything, no matter how disgusting, is something else's lunch. As Jonathan Swift put it, "a flea hath smaller fleas that on him prey; and these have smaller still to bite 'em, and so proceed ad infinitum." Thus losing any plant or creature from what used to be called the Great Chain of Being can have all kinds of unforeseen effects.

"If we allow ourselves to eliminate animals because they don't happen to be attractive to us, then we are acting on emotion rather than on objective criteria," he said. In any event, the peskiest species—like mosquitoes and cockroaches—are far from facing extinction, "I'm sorry to say," he added. 15 "I'm not going to take up the cause of the sewer rat, but there are species for which humans do not hold great affection that may in fact be quite important," said Stephen R. Edwards, executive officer of the Species Survival Commission. "Crocodiles for example." It seems they have an important role in keeping rivers clean.

One idea that will be discussed at Rome is the setting free of animals bred in captivity, which is no easy task, but which has worked in the case of the Arabian oryx. It became extinct in the wild and was reintroduced in Oman from animals kept in zoos.

I. Getting the Message

A. After reading the article, choose the best answer for each item.

1. This article is mostly about
   a. preventing animals from eating people
   b. saving endangered species
   c. destroying fearsome animals

2. In Bengal, workers at the tiger reserves wear masks to
   a. scare the tigers
   b. confuse the tigers
   c. look like tigers

3. Specialists were meeting in Rome to decide
   a. which animals to eliminate
   b. whether to set up a new wildlife organization
   c. how to protect endangered animals

4. According to this article, we should try to prevent any animal species from becoming extinct because
   a. every animal probably improves life on earth in some way
   b. some animals do a lot of harm and no good
   c. all animals are attractive to people

5. The man in the picture has two faces because his mask is on backward. He is also "two-faced" because he
   a. deceives or tricks
   b. walks both ways at once
   c. walks backward

Check your answers with the key on page 170. If you made mistakes, reread the article to gain a better understanding of it.

B. The article mentions many animals. Each is mentioned to illustrate a point the article is making. For example, the tiger illustrates how humans have found a way to protect themselves from an animal they are protecting. Find the point that each animal illustrates. Reread the paragraph shown in parentheses.

1. stink badger (6) _____

2. condor (11) _____

3. crocodile (15) _____

II. Expanding Your Vocabulary

Getting Meaning from Context

Use context clues to determine the meaning of each word or phrase, found
in the paragraph indicated in parentheses. Choose the correct definition.

1. habitats (4):
   a. areas animals live in
   b. bad habits of humans

2. specialists (5):
   a. important people
   b. experts in a particular field of study

3. casualty rate (7):
   a. casual, risky behavior
   b. the amount of injury and death

4. friction (7):
   a. trouble, disagreement
   b. the rubbing together of two things

5. doubled (8):
   a. became twice as much
   b. became half as much

6. launched (8):
   a. begun
   b. sent up into the air

7. priorities (9):
   a. expensive things to do
   b. activities to do sooner than other less important things

8. objective criteria (14):
   a. small objects and creatures
   b. standards of judgment that are free from personal feelings

III. Working with Idioms

Study the meanings of these idioms and expressions.

Phrasal verbs:

draw up (6) = write a document

die out (12) = disappear, become extinct

take up a cause (15) = begin to support a particular idea

set free (16) = let a person or animal out of captivity

Other expressions from the article:

two-faced (1) = deceitful, dishonest

get off someone's back (1) = stop bothering the person

therein lies a tale (1) = it's an interesting story

a losing battle (4) = efforts to do something are failing

beasties (6); **varmints** (10) = slang for animals

dig into their pockets (10) = give money

ad infinitum (13) = Latin for to infinity; endlessly

Complete these sentences, using the idioms and expressions.

1. When someone asks for money to help maintain genetic diversity, people should _____.

2. Some people who are worried about endangered species never stop talking about the problem. They go on about it _____.

3. Endangered species are sometimes kept in a zoo for a while, and then some of the animals are _____ in the hope that they will survive in the wild.

4. Although people are making efforts, many animal species continue to _____.

IV. Analyzing Paragraphs

Paragraphs usually have one main or key idea. Match each of these main ideas with one of these paragraphs: 4, 10, 11 and 15.

Main Idea	Paragraph Number
1. Sometimes endangered species become extinct despite the efforts of those who want to save them.	
2. It's not a good idea to spend a lot of money in an effort to save one species.	
3. People are not eager to give money to save animals that they don't like.	
4. Some species that people consider disgusting or frightening are also useful because they improve the environment in some way.	

Now reread paragraph 16, and write its main idea in your own words.

V. Talking and Writing

A. Discuss the meaning of the title of this article.

B. Discuss the following topics. Then choose one of them to write about.

1. In your native country, are there any endangered species that scientists are trying to save? What is being done to prevent their extinction? Why is it important to save these particular plants or animals?

2. Have you ever taken up a cause that you felt would improve the world? What did you do to influence people to care about your cause?

Science and Environment

Gallbladder Takes a Bow

Previewing the Article

Today video cameras seem to be everywhere. They're hard at work in TV studios, taping humor, romance and violence for mass entertainment. They're monitoring crime in stores, banks and apartment buildings. They're on the streets, taping news in action. They're in the hands of amateur photographers who want to preserve important moments in their lives. They're even in the operating room, assisting with surgery.

In this article, the video camera has an important role. In the high-tech surgical procedure described, the camera goes inside the patient's body to focus on her gallbladder. The camera brings a picture to a TV screen, and that picture is the surgeon's view of the surgical field. Then, because the patient has a wonderful sense of humor, this surgical video becomes home entertainment!

The title—"Gallbladder Takes a Bow"—introduces a comparison that makes the article funny. In this article, the gallbladder is not only an internal organ of the human body; it is also the star of a TV show.

Before You Read

Before you read the article, discuss these questions.
1. Where is the gallbladder? What is its function? Why is it sometimes removed? Do you know anyone who has had this surgery?

2. Have you had any experience with laparoscopy, laser surgery or other high-tech medical procedures?

3. Have you ever had any kind of surgery? Were you unconscious during the operation? Did you have confidence in your surgeon? Were you worried?

As You Read

As you read the article, mark the parts you consider funny. Later, ask yourself why these areas made you smile.

Gallbladder Takes a Bow

Latest in Home TV: Your Very Own Operation

By John Tierney
New York Times Service

NEW YORK—As she put out the popcorn and potato chips in her living room, Karen Bennett said she believed hers was going to be the first party ever held to watch a gallbladder operation. That is a difficult claim to verify. But at the very least it was the first party ever held to watch Karen Bennett's gallbladder operation.

"I can't exactly say I'm excited about it," said Meg Marshall, one of the first guests to arrive at Ms. Bennett's home in the New York suburb of Wantagh last week. "But I'm looking forward to it. Normally I hate looking at other people's home movies, but this will be different."

The guests were promised a videotape of Ms. Bennett's gallbladder in color, magnified 16 times, accompanied by live play-by-play commentary from surgeons as they removed it. The video was recorded two weeks ago by a tiny camera lowered inside her abdomen to guide the surgeons.

This camera, the laparoscope, has revolutionized abdominal surgery in the last several years, but it is probably too early to gauge its impact on home entertainment. Surgeons across the country have begun giving out videotapes, and some medical experts think it is comforting for patients and their friends to see what happens during an operation, but other authorities are skeptical.

5 Letitia Baldrige, who in "Letitia Baldrige's Complete Guide to the New Manners for the 90s" recommends that one's surgery never be discussed for longer than two minutes, reacted to the idea of the party with several pained pauses.

"Oh ohh ohhh," she said, "Well, it's a free country, and people can do what they want. Let me just say that I hope the food is delicious and that it's served well in advance of the screening."

Ms. Bennett, 22, a financial planner who lives with her parents, said that the invitations drew two basic responses.

"One was," she said, "'That sounds really interesting. What time do I come?' The other was, 'Eeew, gross. I'm not going near your house.' I can understand it, because I'm kind of squeamish about these things myself. I wasn't sure if I could watch it. But my curiosity got to me, and I found it wasn't so bad."

Her videotape was an indication of how far the genre has evolved since the first video cameras were used by enthusiastic fathers to record childbirth. Many doctors originally opposed it, fearing the evidence could be used against them in malpractice suits. Today it is often the doctors doing the taping.

10 "A good percentage of our surgeons tape the operations," said Paul Wetter, chairman of the Society of Laparoendoscopic Surgeons, "and many of them give the tapes to their patients. The tapes can help avoid false litigation by showing exactly what happened during surgery. They also build rapport with patients, and that helps avoid litigation, too."

Ms. Bennett's surgeon, Jeffrey Sherwood, said that he routinely taped operations for patients, both to satisfy their curiosity and assuage their fears about what goes on.

Ms. Bennett's tape began with stock footage of Dr. Sherwood at his desk explaining laparoscopic techniques: "This is truly surgery of the future. It is Star Wars and Star Trek rolled into one."

The scene shifted abruptly to Ms. Bennett's abdominal cavity. The image was remarkably clear, thanks to the special camera and light lowered through the navel, and Dr. Sherwood provided a guided tour as he operated. The sound track was recorded while he watched a video screen and manip-

ulated the long handles of miniature instruments inserted into the abdomen through tubes the size of pencils.

"You can see here is the liver," he said as the tiny forceps reached for a brown blob. The forceps lifted the blob and grabbed a gray object underneath. "This is the gallbladder over here which I'm grasping."

15 The star's appearance drew appreciative murmurs from the audience, which consisted of Ms. Bennett's parents, her sister and three friends.

"It looks like a blowfish."

"It's like a balloon."

"Karen, can you believe that's the inside of you?"

The forceps poked around on screen. "We can see over here, Karen, what looks like the artery," Dr. Sherwood said, and his casual tone set off worried commentary from the home audience.

20 "Well, this is not a hit or miss thing—either it is the artery or it isn't." There was more concern when it came time to seal tissue by burning it with an instrument called the cautery.

"It's like a soldering iron."

"Her body is smoking!"

"And you feel none of that, Karen?"

"I'm unconscious," Ms. Bennett explained. "My screen debut, and I'm unconscious."

25 "O.K., Karen," Dr. Sherwood said, "as you can see, the gallbladder is almost off. And there it is, all off. You can see I have the gallbladder now, Karen, and we're going to start to take it out."

The gallbladder exit was accompanied by a whooshing sound as it was sucked off the screen and up a tube. Then came a climactic bit of cinematography; the abdomen rapidly receding from view as the camera pulled out of the body and then panned across the operating table to the gallbladder sitting on a white cloth.

"O.K., Karen, as you can see, here is the gallbladder," Dr. Sherwood said. "We're going to open the gallbladder for you and show you the inside. And there it is."

Everyone applauded. "The human body is so wonderful," said Donna Russell as the video ended.

Dr. Sherwood said that the videos

pleased most of his patients and seemed to help them recuperate. Hilliard Jason, a psychiatrist at the University of Colorado School of Medicine who trains physicians how to communicate with patients, agreed that the videos had promise.

30 "If patients are suitably prepared," Dr. Jason said, "a videotape can probably be useful in demystifying medicine. It removes the veil and tells the patient: 'We're confident in what we're doing, and you should be confident, too.' "

This did not impress Ms. Bald-rige, the authority on etiquette. "There's too much self-absorption today," she said. "When I was a kid, they used to hand us our appendix in a jar after the operation, and I would say that 90 percent of the people threw it away—and it was a better world."

I. Getting the Message

A. After reading the article, choose the best answer for each item.

1. The surgeon in the article put a camera inside Karen
   a. because Karen wanted a videotape of her surgery
   b. so that he could operate by watching the TV picture
   c. because Karen was the first patient that ever had laparoscopic surgery

2. The surgeon was talking to Karen during the operation because
   a. Karen was awake and very frightened
   b. Karen was watching the videotape during the surgery
   c. the surgeon knew that Karen would watch the videotape after the surgery

3. Karen Bennett's gallbladder was
   a. examined and repaired
   b. surgically removed
   c. given to Karen to take home

4. How did Karen feel about her surgery? She
   a. had painful memories and wanted to forget about it
   b. had a lot of curiosity about her operation
   c. was angry because her surgeon videotaped it

5. Letitia Baldrige is
   a. a friend of Karen's
   b. an expert on how to act in social situations
   c. an authority on medical matters

6. Baldrige's opinion on showing a videotape of surgery at a party is that
   a. it's acceptable if food is not served
   b. it's OK if the video is short
   c. one's surgery should not be shown

Check your answers with the key on page 170. If you have made mistakes, reread the article to gain a better understanding of it.

B. List three reasons why surgeons sometimes videotape surgery. List the numbers of the paragraphs that give the reasons.

II. Expanding Your Vocabulary

A. Getting Meaning from Context

Use context clues to determine the meaning of each word, found in the paragraph indicated in parentheses. Choose the correct definition.

1. verify (1):   a. make   b. find proof for
2. magnified (3):   a. shown in larger size   b. praised
3. revolutionized (4): a. overthrew a government   b. greatly changed a procedure
4. gauge (4):   a. determine the extent of   b. find the length of
5. indication (9):   a. direction to take   b. sign of something happening
6. good (10):   a. fairly large part   b. the best
7. rapport (10):   a. a very close friendship   b. a relationship of mutual understanding
8. climactic (26):   a. relating to temperature   b. most exciting, dramatic point

B. Reading for Suggested Meanings

Answer these questions.

1. In paragraph 4, other authorities are described as *skeptical*. Does this mean that they agree with showing videotapes or that they question the worth of the practice?
2. In paragraph 6, Letitia Baldrige reacts with *pained pauses*. The phrase doesn't mean that she was in pain, but it suggests her reaction to videotaping surgery. What is her position?
3. In paragraph 9, the word *genre* is used. It usually means a kind of art form. Why is it appropriate here?
4. In paragraph 9, doctors thought that ". . . the evidence [videotapes] could be used against them in malpractice suits." Does this mean that videotapes might show the mistakes surgeons made or that the patients may sue surgeons for videotaping operations?
5. In paragraph 15, the *star's* appearance is mentioned. Who is the star?

C. Finding the Word That Doesn't Belong

Circle the word that doesn't fit into each category.

1. **surgical instruments:**
    laparoscope   forceps   navel   cautery
2. **organs of the body:**
    liver   appendix   etiquette   gallbladder
3. **words used in videotaping:**
    scene   sound track   footage   curiosity
4. **careers in medicine:**
    surgeon   financial analyst   psychiatrist   physician
5. **words related to entertainment:**
    applaud   star   blob   audience

III. Working with Idioms

Study the meanings of these idioms and expressions.

take a bow (from the headline) = to receive praise for good work

look forward to (2) = expect (usually something nice); be eager for

play-by-play (3) = description of an event while it is happening

give out (4) = distribute, hand out

gross (8) = a slang expression for disgusting

kind of (8) = rather, sort of (slang)

set off (19) = start, cause something to start

hit or miss (20) = carelessly done

have promise (29) = have a good chance of success

remove the veil (30) = reveal something not understood well before

Complete these sentences with the idioms and expressions.

1. Karen probably didn't _____ having an operation.
2. She chose a surgeon who was very careful. He didn't do a _____ job.
3. While the surgeon was operating on Karen, he also gave a _____ description of the surgery.
4. Some people think that watching surgery is _____.
5. Watching a videotape of a surgical procedure helps to _____ of mystery and allows patients to understand it better.

IV. Focusing on Style and Tone

Comparison and contrast is one common way that writers develop ideas.
Answer these questions about comparisons in the article.

1. What is the contrast between Ms. Baldrige and the physicians who are quoted in the article?
2. According to the author, the patient is making her "debut," and the gallbladder is the "star" of the show. What is the author comparing this operation to? Why is the comparison appropriate?

V. Talking and Writing

Discuss the following topics. Then choose one of them to write about.

1. This article suggests that many problems can arise in the doctor-patient relationship. What are some of them?
2. Have you ever watched an operation being performed, either live or on TV? If so, what did you see, and how did you feel about it? If not, would you like to? What if you were the patient?
3. What do you think of the idea of parties to show surgery videotapes? Would you go to one? Would you give one?

Science and Environment

Dolphins Display Cunning and Brutality in Courtship

Previewing the Article

It's always a good story when new scientific discoveries disprove a popular idea. In this article, the public is forced to reconsider the personality and character of the supposedly lovable dolphin. According to recent studies, dolphins have a darker, meaner side. The battle between the sexes can become physically violent among dolphins. But not everything we once "knew" about dolphins is wrong. As you read the article, you will learn something about the social skills of dolphins.

Before You Read

Before you read the article, discuss these questions.
1. Have you ever seen dolphins perform? What do they look like? What tricks can they do?
2. What do you know about dolphins? What image do you have of them?

As You Read

As you read, look for reasons why dolphins behave as they do. How do their social skills and group life help them survive?

Dolphins Display Cunning and Brutality in Courtship

'Gangs' Conspire to Steal Females of Their Rivals

© Alice M. Prescott/Unicorn Stock Photos

Frolicking dolphins seem happy and carefree, but studies reveal that they are clever enough to form sophisticated alliances and can be aggressive.

By Natalie Angier
New York Times Service

NEW YORK—As much as puppies or pandas or even children, dolphins are universally beloved. They seem to cavort and frolic at the least provocation, their mouths are fixed in what looks like a state of perpetual merriment, and their behavior and enormous brains suggest an intelligence approaching that of humans—or even, some might argue, surpassing it.

Dolphins are turning out to be exceedingly clever, but not in the loving, utopian-socialist manner that sentimental dolphin lovers might have hoped.

Researchers who have spent thousands of hours observing the behavior of bottlenose dolphins off the coast of Australia have discovered that the males form social alliances with one another that are far more sophisticated and devious than any seen in animals apart from human beings.

They have found that one team of male dolphins will recruit the help of another team of males to gang up against a third group, a sort of multitiered battleplan that scientists said requires considerable mental calculus to work out.

5   But the purpose of these complex alliances is not exactly sportive. Males

They seem to be far more sophisticated and devious than other animals.

collude with their peers as a way of stealing fertile females from competing dolphin bands.

And after they have succeeded in

spiriting a female away, the males remain in their tight-knit group to assure that the female stays in line, performing a series of feats that are at once spectacular and threatening.

Two or three males will surround the female, leaping and bellyflopping, swiveling and somersaulting, all in perfect synchrony with one another. Should the female be so unimpressed as to attempt to flee, the males will chase after her, bite her, slap her with their fins or slam into her with their bodies.

The scientists call this effort to control females "herding," but they acknowledge that the word does not convey the aggressiveness of the act.

"Sometimes the female is obviously trying to escape, and the noises start to sound like they're hurting each other," said Dr. Rachel A. Smolker of the University of Michigan in Ann Arbor. "The hitting sounds hards, and the female may end up with tooth-rake marks."

10   Dr. Smolker, Dr. Andrew F. Richards and Dr. Richard C. Connor, who is now at the Woods Hole Oceanographic Institution in Massachusetts, reported their findings about dolphin alliances and herding in the Proceedings of the National Academy of Sciences.

The researchers said that, while marine biologists have long been impressed with the intelligence and social complexity of bottlenose dolphins, they were surprised by the intricacy of the males' machinations.

Many male primates, including chimpanzees and baboons, are known to form into gangs to attack rival camps, but scientists have never before seen one group of animals soliciting a second to go after a third.

More impressive, the two-part alliances among dolphins seem to be extremely flexible, shifting from day to day depending on the dolphins' needs, whether or not one group owes a favor to another, and the dolphins' perceptions of what they can get away with.

The animals seem to be highly opportunistic, which means that each must always be computing who is friend and who is foe.

15   "If you think of an interaction between groups that is predictably hostile, it doesn't seem to require much gray matter to know where you stand," said Dr. Connor. "But when you have situations always changing between alliances, you get the soap opera effect. 'What did he do with her today?' 'Should we go after them tomorrow?' "

The biologists also have evidence that females form sophisticated alliances in an effort to thwart male encroachment, and that bands of females will chase after an alliance of males that has stolen one of their friends from the fold.

What is more, females seem to exert choice over the males that seek to herd them, sometimes swimming alongside them in apparent contentment, but at other times working furiously to escape, and often succeeding.

But female dolphin behavior is usually more subtle than the male theatrics, and hence less easily deciphered, particularly under the difficult field conditions of studying animals that spend much of their time underwater.

Dr. Connor and others suggest that the demands of intricate and ever-changing social allegiances and counter-allegiances could have been the force driving the evolution of intelligence among dolphins.

20   "The smarter some animals get, and the greater their ability to form and use alliances, the more important it is for other animals to get as smart," said Dr. Richard W. Wrangham, a professor of anthropology at Harvard University who has studied social behavior among primates.

"This could be the sort of selective pressure one is looking for to explain the evolution of the dolphin's brain," he added.

Most of the 30 species of dolphins and small whales are extremely social, forming into schools of anywhere from several to hundreds of mammals, which periodically break off into smaller clans and then come back together again in what is called a fission-fusion society.

Their sociality seems to help them evade sharks and to forage for fish more effectively.

Species like the bottlenose and the spinner dolphins make most of their decisions by consensus, spending hours dawdling in a protected bay, nuzzling each other and generating an eerie nautical symphony of squeaks, whistles, barks, twangs and clicks.

25   But dolphins become particularly churlish when they want to mate, or to avoid being mated. Female bottlenose dolphins bear a single calf only once every four or five years, so a fertile female is a prized commodity to the males.

Because there is almost no size difference between the sexes, a single female cannot be forced to mate by a lone male. That may be part of the reason why males team into gangs.

I. Getting the Message

A. After reading the article, choose the best answer for each item.

1. The popular image of dolphins is that they are
   a. happy and intelligent
   b. aggressive and intelligent
   c. social and timid

2. Like many primates such as chimpanzees, groups of dolphins join together to
   a. make tools
   b. attack rival groups
   c. find new territories

3. Unlike alliances now known among primates such as chimpanzees, the alliances that dolphins form
   a. are more aggressive
   b. can involve two groups joining together to attack another group
   c. are more permanent

4. According to Wrangham, the smarter animals get,
   a. the more aggressive they are
   b. the more tools they use
   c. the more sophisticated alliances they can form

5. The sociality of dolphins helps them to
   a. find food more effectively
   b. do tricks
   c. mate more frequently

Check your answers with the key on page 170. If you have made mistakes, reread the article to gain a better understanding of it.

B. All of these statements are about dolphins.

■ Some express ideas that people used to believe about dolphins but that scientists now know are false. Write *F* for them.

■ Some state new information about dolphins gained from recent studies. Write *N* for them.

■ Some are facts known in the past and confirmed by recent studies. Write *C* for them.

_____ 1. Dolphins are always peaceful and friendly.
_____ 2. Dolphins have good social skills.
_____ 3. Dolphins are very smart.
_____ 4. Alliances between groups of male dolphins can change from day to day.
_____ 5. Female dolphins organize to rescue a kidnapped friend.

■ II. Expanding Your Vocabulary

Getting Meaning from Context

Use context clues to determine the meaning of each word or phrase, found in the paragraph indicated in parentheses. Choose the correct definition.

1. merriment (1):
   a. state of being full of fun and laughter
   b. state of constant movement

2. collude (5):
   a. run into and hit
   b. act together to do something against someone

3. spiriting away (6):
   a. stealing someone's soul or spirit
   b. kidnapping or stealing someone or something

4. soliciting (12):
   a. asking for help
   b. constantly bothering

5. counter-allegiances (19):
   a. loyalties formed to fight against other groups
   b. an attack against friends

6. sociality (23):
   a. a kind of gathering
   b. tendency to be in groups

7. consensus (24):
   a. majority rule
   b. general agreement

8. churlish (25):
   a. rude and bad-tempered
   b. sociable and friendly

III. Working with Idioms

Study the meanings of these idioms and expressions.

Phrasal verbs:
turn out (2) = end up, be a particular way in the end
work out (4) = find a solution to
get away with (13) = do something inappropriate and not get caught or punished
break off (22) = separate from
come back (22) = return
Other expressions:
stay in line (6) = follow the rules or orders
gray matter (15) = brains, intelligence

Complete these sentences, using the idioms and expressions. Use the correct verb tenses.

1. Male dolphins try to steal females from another group. Sometimes they _____ it, but sometimes the female's friends come and rescue her.
2. In recent research, dolphins have _____ to be very intelligent. They have a lot of _____.
3. Dolphins have a fission-fusion society because small groups _____ and then _____ again.

IV. Making Sense of Sentences

To develop her ideas, this author uses comparison and contrast in three ways. Dolphins are compared to other animals, and male dolphins are compared to females. In addition, past ideas about dolphins are compared and contrasted to recent discoveries.

Complete the comparisons in these sentences by filling in either (1) a short comparative adjective ending with *-er* or (2) the word *more* or *less* plus an adjective. Look in the paragraphs indicated for the facts you need.

Example: Perhaps dolphins are *more intelligent* than human beings. (1)

1. This article tells readers that dolphins are _____ than previously thought. (2)
2. The social alliances of dolphins are _____ than scientists realized in the past. (3)
3. The alliances of chimpanzees are _____ than those of dolphins. (3, 12)
4. Scientists say that female dolphins are _____ to understand than males. (18)

V. Talking and Writing

Discuss the following topics. Then choose one of them to write about.

1. Do you think any of the animals that people commonly have as pets are capable of caring about and loving their owners? Give evidence to support your point of view.
2. Scientists work hard to learn more about the social behavior of dolphins. What is the value of this knowledge? Do you think it is useful or merely interesting?

Science and Environment

The Latest Riddle of the Sphinx

Previewing the Article

"How old are you?" That should be an easy question to answer, but not when scientists are asking it of the world-famous Great Sphinx of Egypt. The Sphinx remains silent, keeping its secret. But a range of specialists— archaeologists, geologists, geophysicists and engineers—are using high-tech science to try to determine its age.

For some readers, the headline on this article may raise three questions: (1) What's a sphinx? (2) What's a riddle? and (3) What was the original riddle of the sphinx?

The sphinx, an imaginary animal, was created by ancient cultures and used in their art and literature. In some folklore, the sphinx had the head of a human being, a bird, or a goat and the body of a lion. The oldest, largest and most well-known sculpture of a sphinx lies in a desert near Giza, Egypt. It is called the Great Sphinx. For thousands of years, it has guarded the tombs of the pharaohs (Egyptian kings). The Great Sphinx has a human face and the Egyptian royal headdress, over the body of a lion.

The riddle (puzzling question) of the sphinx comes from ancient Greek mythology. The sphinx lived on a high rock just outside the ancient city of Thebes, asking anyone who passed this riddle:

"What goes on four legs in the morning, on two at noon and on three in the evening?" None of the passersby could answer, and the sphinx killed them all. Then Oedipus solved the riddle and ended the reign of terror. Can you solve it? The answer is printed in the box on page 143.

Before You Read

Before you read the article, discuss these questions.
1. Have you ever visited Egypt and seen the Great Sphinx? If so, describe it and the nearby pyramids.
2. What mythological creatures are you familiar with from your native culture or others you have studied?

As You Read

The words *erosion* and *weathering*, both used in this article, refer to the gradual wearing away of the earth's surface as the result of natural processes. Weathering is erosion caused by weather-related forces such as wind, wind-blown sand, rain, snow, floods and waves. As you read, look for information about how the weathering of the Great Sphinx provides clues to its age.

The Latest Riddle of the Sphinx

The ancient Sphinx, pictured here being restored, may be thousands of years older than previously thought.

By John Noble Wilford
New York Times Service

NEW YORK—Unwrapping an enigma to find the riddle inside, geologists studying the Great Sphinx of Egypt have found patterns of weathering and erosion that they say show the imposing monument was created thousands of years earlier than is generally thought.

Robert M. Schoch, a Boston University geologist who directed the research, reported that an ancient civilization carved the Sphinx between 5000 B.C. and 7000 B.C., long before the dynasties of pharoahs. Archaeologists have long contended that it was built by Pharaoh Khafre about 2500 B.C.

Schoch suggested that Khafre had merely restored the Sphinx, a mythological creature with the body of a lion and a human head, and perhaps made some alterations. The monument, 66 feet high and 240 feet long (about 20 by 74 meters), stands at Giza with the Great Pyramids.

The research findings were announced Wednesday at the annual meeting of the Geological Society of America in San Diego. They immediately drew fire from Mark Lehner, an Egyptologist at the University of Chicago who is a leading expert on the Sphinx.

5   The Associated Press quoted Lehner as saying there was "overwhelming evidence," including samples of rock from the same quarry used for the Sphinx and other monuments at the site, to support Khafre's role in the construction. Lehner was traveling in Egypt and could not be reached for further comment.

In a telephone interview, Schoch defended his research methods, which involved the use of sound waves to probe subsurface rock and identify the depth and the distinctive pattern of weathering attributed to water.

He worked with Thomas L. Dobecki, a geophysicist at McBride-Ratcliff & Associates, a seismic surveying concern in Houston, and John Anthony West, an independent Egyptologist who had developed the theory that the Sphinx was much older than archaeologists had said.

If their findings are substantiated by other research, archaeologists may have to revise their interpretations of the Middle East before the rise of Egyptian civilization in about 3000 B.C.

Little is known of these Neolithic cultures, but if some were capable of engineering projects on the scale of the

Sphinx, then they can no longer be viewed as simple hunters and gatherers.

10   The massive stone wall and tower of Jericho, dating back to the 9th millennium B.C., are among the few artifacts in the region that tend to support the notion that some of these early cultures might have been capable of conceiving and executing a construction project on the scale of the Sphinx.

Schoch, an associate professor of science, said that subsurface limestone at the front and sides of the Sphinx showed structural signs of water weathering as deep as six to eight feet. Limestone at the back of the Sphinx, carved from the same bedrock, shows weathering only four feet deep.

"The dramatic weathering we found on the body of the Sphinx is not seen on other structures in the immediate vicinity," Schoch said, "even though many of them appear to have been cut or built from very similar or identical limestones and are supposed to have been built during the same period."

Schoch said this suggested that at first the front of the body and head of the Sphinx were carved free from the surrounding bedrock. The rear of the creature remained merged with the surrounding rock.

It is a "reasonable hypothesis," Schoch said, that Khafre repaired and refurbished the Sphinx and the two nearby temples, the Sphinx Temple and the Valley Temple, and also had the back, or western end, of the Sphinx carved out and freed from the cliff.

15   Since the monument was built by excavating surrounding limestone, exposing the core out of which the Sphinx was carved, the rock floor has

© Robert Frerck/Odyssey Productions/Chicago

If the new research proves true, the Sphinx is much older than the surrounding pyramids.

presumably been exposed directly to weathering since the construction began.

The patterns, Schoch said, had all the marks of being "precipitation induced" weathering.

And since the effects were detectable at such great depths, he said, it indicated that work on the Sphinx had begun in the period between 10,000 B.C. and 5,000 B.C., when the Egyptian climate was wetter.

I. Getting the Message

A. After reading the article, indicate if each item is true (*T*) or false (*F*).

_____   1.   The latest scientific research shows that the Great Sphinx is much younger than experts previously thought.

_____   2.   Geologist Robert Schoch believes that the Great Sphinx was built at least 7,000 years ago.

_____   3.   In order to determine the age of the rock inside the Sphinx, scientists had to drill holes in it.

_____ 4. By studying the depth of the weathering caused by water, scientists are trying to find out when the Sphinx was carved.

_____ 5. The weathering patterns found on the front of the Sphinx resemble those on nearby stone structures.

_____ 6. One hypothesis is that the carving of the Sphinx was finished several centuries after it was begun.

_____ 7. Schoch's theories about the age of the Sphinx have been confirmed by later research.

_____ 8. The importance of Schoch's theory is that our ideas about the achievements of early civilizations may change.

Check your answers with the key on page 170. If you have made mistakes, reread the article to gain a better understanding of it.

B. What is the importance of these dates?

3000 B.C. _____

5000–7000 B.C. _____

9000 B.C. _____

II. Expanding Your Vocabulary

A. *Getting Meaning from Context*

Use context clues to determine the meaning of each word, found in the paragraph indicated in parentheses. Choose the correct definition.

1. enigma (1):   a. puzzling question   b. small piece of sculpture
2. contended (2):   a. agreed   b. argued
3. mythological (3):   a. modern   b. taken from legends
4. overwhelming (5)   a. very much   b. surprising
5. revise (8):   a. visit someone again   b. change something, but not completely
6. dramatic (12):   a. important and very noticeable b. theatrical
7. merged (13):   a. under   b. combined with
8. presumably (15):   a. supposedly   b. certainly
9. detectable (17):   a. capable of being discovered b. buried

B. *Studying Word Parts*

Match each underlined word part with its definition.

1. archae<u>o</u>logist   _____ a person who studies
2. Egypto<u>logist</u>   _____ under, below, beneath
3. <u>ex</u>cavating, <u>ex</u>posing _____ ancient, the beginning
4. <u>geo</u>logist   _____ speech, story, legend
5. <u>myth</u>ological   _____ earth, of the earth
6. <u>sub</u>surface   _____ out, from, away from

III. Making Sense of Sentences

Some statements that include an *if* clause are about a possibility, something that could happen in the future.

If it rains tomorrow, we won't take a walk.

Other *if* statements are about imagining that something impossible (or not true) happened or could happen.

If I had four hands, I could do a lot more work.

Reread the *if* statements in paragraphs 8 and 9. Are they telling about something possible or impossible?

Complete these *if* statements about the Sphinx.

1. If Robert Schoch is correct, _____.
2. If Mark Lehner is correct, _____.
3. If archaeologists knew which pharaoh built the Sphinx, _____.
4. If the Sphinx had been made of wood or clay, _____.
5. If I ever take a trip to Egypt, _____.

Which of the five statements above are about possibilities?

IV. Talking and Writing

A. Do you know any riddles? If so, tell one to the class.

B. Discuss the following topics. Then choose one of them to write about.

1. In your native country, are there any very old structures that people come to see? Choose one and tell what and where it is, how and when it was built and why people find it interesting today.

2. What scientific or historical puzzles do you know about? How are scientists or other specialists trying to solve them? Examples would be the origin of old structures or monuments and how they were built. Why do you think these puzzles interest people? Are they worth the effort to solve?

> **Answer to the riddle of the Sphinx:**
> Man, who crawls as a child, walks erect in manhood
> and uses a cane in old age.

FOCUS ON THE NEWSPAPER

Science and Environment

Analyzing Science Articles; Articles on Ecology and Health Care

Newspapers print articles on science topics when the information is of interest or importance to the general public. Many articles report the results of research: for example, scientists may have discovered a way to produce energy from the atom or from the sun more effectively or have made a breakthrough in research on a disease.

Explanations in Science Articles

The journalist must be careful to make the technical material meaningful to readers who are not specialists in the field. Science-related articles often include definitions, examples, comparisons, reasons and statistics (numerical facts) to help readers understand the scientific findings.

Exercise 1: Dissecting a Science Article

Find a science article in the daily newspaper. Number the paragraphs in the article. Then read it, looking for the information requested in the chart.

Analysis of a Science Article			
Main idea:			
Did you find . . .	Yes	No	Paragraph number(s)
1. a definition?			
2. an example?			
3. a comparison?			
4. a reason?			
5. a result?			
6. a statistic?			
7. a problem?			
8. a solution?			
9. a scientific discovery?			
10. a recommendation?			
11. contrasting points of view?			

Articles on Ecology

Ecology is that branch of science that deals with the relationship between living things and their environment. In recent years, there has been a lot of public concern about the environment throughout the world. Newspapers frequently print articles about air, water and land pollution and about damage to plants and animals. These articles can be divided into two main categories: (1) those that tell about present or future harm; and (2) those that tell about efforts to improve the environment.

Exercise 2: Articles on Our Environment

Find a newspaper article on the general topic of ecology. Then answer these questions about it.

1. What is the main idea of this article? State it in one sentence.
2. Who or what is affected by the problem?
3. Does this article make you feel optimistic or pessimistic about the environment on earth in the future?
4. What is the source of the information in the article?
5. Do you think this is an objective source, or would this person, group, business, industry and so on, have a bias? Would self-interest be served by making things sound better or worse than they really are?

Articles on Health Care

Newspapers often print news stories about the latest in medical research and treatment. Many papers also print regular columns by physicians and other health care experts. These answer questions from readers and give advice about physical and mental health.

Daily newspapers are an important source of information about advances in the field of medicine. Newspapers perform a great service by telling people how to take better care of themselves.

Exercise 3: It's Your Health

Scan the headlines of three newspapers, and look for articles and columns about health care. Select two articles or columns to read and analyze. Then write down this information about each article:

1. What is the most important scientific fact stated in the article?
2. Did you know this fact before reading it here?
3. Is there a stated or implied recommendation about changing behavior to stay or become healthier (for example, avoid smoking or eating fats)?

Sports

Sports

A Chinese Tennis Player's Uneasy Season

Previewing the Article

"Keeping your eye on the ball" isn't easy when there is political strife in your native land. However, a young tennis pro, Hu Na, must do just that to compete in tournaments and earn a living. Read this article to discover how she keeps her eye on tennis though her mind is on her family and homeland.

The political events in China serve as background to the article. In 1989, there were demonstrations in China for a more democratic government against the current communist regime. The movement was repressed, culminating in a bloody battle in Tiananmen Square, the main plaza in Beijing. As this article shows, the events were not confined to China, but affected the lives of Chinese around the world.

Before You Read

Before you read the article, discuss these questions.
1. What does it take to be a good tennis player?
2. What sport is very popular in your native country? Why do you think that people like it so much?

As You Read

As you read, look for answers to these questions.
1. What is Hu Na's relationship with the Chinese government?
2. How does Hu Na communicate with her parents?

A Chinese Tennis Player's Uneasy Season

By Bud Collins
International Herald Tribune

SAN DIEGO—The televised images from Tiananmen Square were horrible enough. But it was the unknown and unseen happenings in her hometown, Chengdu, that doubly hurt Hu Na.

"I have heard through friends there were demonstrations and killings there, too, but they didn't get publicity," she said. "I hope my family and friends are all right. I haven't heard from them since the demonstrations."

Compared with the rumblings from her homeland, the tennis career of Hu—the first, and only, Chinese professional player—is secondary these days.

"When I'm playing I'm concentrating on tennis," she said. "I have to. But I hope I hear from my parents soon."

5   For a while after she defected to the United States in 1982, Hu was an embarrassment to the Chinese government and her line of communication with home was severed.

"But things got better," said Hu, who lives in San Diego. "We could talk by phone. My parents would go to the post office and call me. But not since the demonstrations.

"One thing worries me now. I was in some protests against the Chinese government in California a little while ago."

"If I was recognizable on TV," she added, "maybe they know about it at home. I hope that doesn't make it hard for my family."

A player with an aggressive style, Hu savors grass. Last month, at a grass tournament in Newport, Rhode Island, she had her best singles performance of the year, a quarterfinal finish, which raised her ranking to 90th in the world. Her highest ranking ever was in 1987, when she was ranked 53d.

10   The week after the Newport tournament, Hu teamed with Michelle Jaggard of Australia to win the doubles title at a tournament in Schenectady, New York. It was her first professional title.

And she says that she is "still improving."

At 26, she is a middle-level perfor-

UPI/BETTMAN

These days it's not easy for Hu Na to keep her eye on the ball.

mer with only a handful of name victims on her resumé, such as Natalia Zvereva and Kathy Rinaldi. But she can nonetheless claim one championship title: the 1982 Chinese singles title.

"But," she concedes, there are "not many players there."

Hu said she has been "working hard" on both her tennis and on learning English.

15   "I learned a lot from watching TV," she said. Then one day I say, 'Oh, gosh, now I can speak.' A very good feeling."

Despite relatively little financial success (about $12,000 in 1989 prize money), she says she is "doing fine as a pro."

She attributes this in part to her sponsorship by a Taiwan racket manufacturer, whose president "has been very kind."

"And I have been able to live with Chinese families since settling in the U.S.," she added.

She is proud of her U.S. citizenship, which she attained five months ago.

20   "I was making plans to bring my parents and sister and brother to live here," Hu said. "It was going well. But now, all the trouble. I don't know what will happen, how long it could take.

"I just hope things will be good again. I miss my family very much."

She knows, however, that in her job she must keep her eye on the ball. But too often her vision is blurred by those terrible TV images from home.

▌ I. Getting the Message

A. After reading the article, choose the best answer for each item.

1. Hu's main problem is
   a. becoming a top-rated player
   b. learning English
   c. finding out about her family in China

2. Hu was an embarrassment to China when she
   a. defected in 1982
   b. was sponsored in the United States
   c. played with an aggressive style

3. Hu favors playing tennis
   a. on concrete
   b. on clay
   c. on grass

4. In 1982, Hu was
   a. the Chinese doubles champion
   b. the Chinese singles champion
   c. ranked 53rd

5. In terms of her financial situation, Hu
   a. earns a great deal of money as a tennis professional
   b. depends on money given her by a Taiwan racket manufacturer
   c. gives most of her money to the Chinese government

6. Hu has learned a lot of English by
   a. playing tennis
   b. watching TV
   c. becoming a pro

Check your answers with the key on page 170. If you have made mistakes, reread the article to gain a better understanding of it.

B. Scan the article to find what the importance of these places is in Hu's life. Complete the chart.

Place	Importance
Taiwan	
Tiananmen Square	
San Diego	
Chengdu	
Schenectady, NY	
Newport, RI	

II. Expanding Your Vocabulary

A. Getting Meaning from Context

Use context clues to determine the meaning of each word, found in the paragraph indicated in parentheses. Choose the correct definition.

1. uneasy (1):   a. difficult   b. worried
2. publicity (2):   a. reports about an event on   b. television advertisements
                                television or radio
3. demonstrations (2):   a. explaining something by   b. meetings to protest
                                using samples   political actions
4. concentrating (4):   a. adding a substance   b. paying attention
5. defected (5):   a. failed   b. left without permission
6. savors (9):   a. tastes   b. enjoys
7. resumé (12):   a. summary of experiences   b. notification
8. concedes (13):   a. surrenders   b. accepts as true

B. Defining Useful Vocabulary

Match each word with its definition.

1. attain   _____ a few
2. ranking   _____ attacking
3. aggressive   _____ not the best or the worst
4. middle-level   _____ position in relation to others
5. severed   _____ cut off, stopped
6. a handful   _____ get, reach

C. Practicing Useful Vocabulary

Complete the sentences with words from exercise B.

1. Hu's tennis style is _____. However, on the professional tour, she is only a _____ player.
2. Important events have occurred in Hu's life. On the positive side, she recently was able to _____ U.S. citizenship. But on the negative side, her communication with her family in China has been _____.
3. Hu's _____ among professional tennis players is not very high; however, she has defeated _____ of excellent players.

D. Reading for Suggested Meanings

Answer these questions.

1. In paragraph 3, the author uses the word *rumblings.* The word means both the heavy sound thunder makes and expressions of unhappiness. To what does it refer in the paragraph?

2. In paragraph 12, why did the author choose the word *victims* to describe the players Hu defeated? Do you think such a word is unusual for a sports article?

3. In paragraph 22, *keep your eye on the ball* is an idiom that means "pay attention." What is its double meaning here?

4. In paragraph 22, the author says that Hu's vision is *blurred,* which means she can't see things clearly.
   a. Why is Hu's vision blurred?
   b. How does the word *blurred* relate to the previous sentence in the article?

III. Making Sense of Sentences

Sometimes sentences with two clauses (two subjects and two verbs) are introduced by a word or words at the beginning. Study this sentence from paragraph 8.

If I was recognizable on TV, maybe they know about it at home.

The word *if,* a subordinating conjunction, introduces the first part of the sentence and connects it to the second part. In the space below, complete the sentences from the story.

paragraph 4: When _____

paragraph 5: For a while after _____ government.

Write two sentences of your own about the story. Begin one with *if* and one with *when.*

IV. Talking and Writing

Discuss the following topics. Then choose one of them to write about.

1. Who is the most famous professional athlete in your country? Why is this athlete so popular?

2. Some people like to participate in sports. Others prefer to observe them. What sport do you prefer to participate in or to observe? Give some reasons why you like this sport.

Sports

In Europe, It's Still Diamonds in the Rough

Previewing the Article

Baseball, a relatively unfamiliar sport to Europeans, used to be played only by the rich in France. Now the French, who are hosting the European baseball championships, are trying to create enthusiasm for the game on that continent. They have hired David Daniels to coach their national team. He was once a player for one of America's minor league (or lower-level professional) teams. Now he is responsible for turning an inexperienced French team into "gems of players" on the baseball "diamond" (the shape of a baseball field)—hence, the title of the article you are about to read.

Other developments are also occurring that will increase the popularity of a sport that was first introduced to Europe in Italy during World War II.

Before You Read

Before you read the article, discuss these questions.
1. Has any new sport recently become popular in your native country? Why do you think this sport has become popular in a new cultural context?
2. What is the role of television in popularizing new sports in your native country?

As You Read

As you read, look for answers to these questions.
1. What is the status of baseball in European countries?
2. What are some reasons for Europeans' interest in baseball?

In Europe, It's Still Diamonds in the Rough

By John McMurtrie
International Herald Tribune

PARIS—David Daniels was amazed when he first saw the baseball team he was to coach.

As a retired American minor league player who had coached in Italy and the Netherlands, Daniels had been recruited to help prepare the French national team for the European Baseball Championships that begin Friday in Paris.

What Daniels saw before him was not the makings of a national team. "It was a disaster," he recalled of that first training session last winter in Florida. "I had guys scattered all over the infield who couldn't even catch a ball. And I won't say anything about what it was like when they had a bat in their hands."

Daniels, now, is still hoping for the best as the French will host, for the first time, the European Baseball Championships.

5   As a taste of a sport that is fast gaining popularity in Europe, and will continue to attract attention with baseball becoming a medal sport at the 1992 Olympics in Barcelona, the 21st edition of the biennial championships featured nine days of competition between the eight teams belonging to Group A of the European Confederation of Amateur Baseball (CEBA).

Group B, the second division that includes teams newly joining the CEBA, such as the Soviet Union and Czechoslovakia, also holds its own series every two years.

CEBA officials rate Italy and the Netherlands as the best national teams now in Europe. France, Spain and Belgium will likely vie next week for third place, with Germany, Sweden and Great Britain battling to avoid

Nicolae Asciu

becoming the team that is demoted to Group B.

Baseball has its largest European following, by far, in Italy and the Netherlands. Each has as many as 30,000 amateur players, each has hundreds of baseball fields. France, by contrast, has just put the final touches on its capital's first field.

Aldo Notari, president of both the Italian baseball federation and CEBA, and vice-president of the International Baseball Association, attributes baseball's initial success in Italy to the American presence there during and after World War II.

10   "We opened up to the rest of the world after the war," said Notari. "Baseball was a form of cultural exchange with the Americans. We held on to it and, with good direction, have made it the national sport it is today."

Peter Laanen, president of the Royal Dutch Baseball and Softball Federation, attributed the sport's popularity in his country to promotion.

"If we're getting better at baseball

in Holland," said Laanen, "it's because we know how to sell it and how to educate our audience through the media. The size of our country also lets us reach people more easily."

In France, where baseball is only slowly being discovered, federation officials hope that by hosting the championship they can lower the sport's image.

"Baseball in France used to be a sport of the rich," said Bruno Lesfargues, president of the French federation. "Today, it's attracting people from all classes and is played all over France."

15   Germany's baseball federation also has seen a dramatic increase in the number of those playing the game. A decade ago the federation there consisted of 10 teams; today there are 200. Still, the German and the British federations are the only ones in Europe that do not receive governmental financial backing. That worries the German group's president, Martin Miller, whose main objective in Paris will be

to avoid a demotion to Group B.

"Our biggest problem is money," he said. "Without it, we can't really do more than to hope for a fifth place in the championships."

Although baseball is quickly taking root in Europe, even those involved in the sport are the first to admit that it is not yet popular in most of the 19 countries belonging to CEBA. For those with any ties to the game, learning about baseball had more to do with meeting Americans, Canadians or Asians abroad than it did with taking a turn at bat.

Reto Blum, the Swiss federation's president, recalled first playing baseball when visiting family in the United States as a teen-ager. "My cousin was a Red Sox fan, so I had to be a Yankees fan," he said. "It all started there."

20 While European players have a passion for the game, most think of it as only a hobby. Some have gone on to play in American minor leagues— at least one, pitcher Win Remmerswaal of the Netherlands, made it to the major leagues, with the Boston Red Sox—but their numbers are few. And the European Confederation does not foresee a continental professional league, at least not for years to come.

"If we grow to the point of being able to have a professional league," said the CEBA's president, Notari, "we'll become professional on our own. What we don't want is to be part of a colony of somebody else's pro league. Besides, our focus is on the Olympics."

For most, though, even the Olympics are out of reach. Of the eight teams that played in Barcelona in 1992, three came from Europe, with Spain automatically qualifying as the host nation. The other two teams were to be determined at the 1991 European Championships.

But today's underdogs have not given up hope. Jeff Milleras, a French-Canadian who has played in past championships for the French, is one.

"Maybe it isn't realistic to think we can beat the Italians and Dutch," he said. "But five years ago it was an embarrassment to go out there and play. Now, we're competitive. Others may be better than us, but who knows, this is the sport of miracles."

I. Getting the Message

A. After reading the article, indicate if each item is true (*T*) or false (*F*).

_____ 1. David Daniels was pleased by the high quality of the French team.

_____ 2. Italy and Czechoslovakia have the best European amateur teams.

_____ 3. Most European players think of baseball as a hobby rather than a profession.

_____ 4. The European league hopes to join another nation's professional league.

_____ 5. Baseball's growing popularity in Europe is directly related to the sharp decline in interest in soccer.

_____ 6. A major reason for the growing interest in baseball is that baseball is now a sport in which a country's team can receive an Olympic medal.

Check your answers with the key on page 170. If you have made mistakes, reread the article to gain a better understanding of it.

B. List two reasons for Europeans' growing interest in baseball.

II. Expanding Your Vocabulary

Getting Meaning from Context

Use context clues to determine the meaning of each word, found in the paragraph indicated in parentheses. Choose the correct definition.

1. recruited (2):   a. joined the army   b. engaged for service

2. rate (7):   a. to place in a particular rank   b. to value for taxation

3. promotion (11):   a. advertising   b. advancement at one's work

4. objective (16):   a. uninfluenced by emotion   b. serving as a goal

5. admit (18):   a. agree to be true   b. allow to participate

6. competitive (24): a. capable of winning a contest   b. winning

III.   Working with Idioms

Study the meanings of these idioms and expressions.

the makings of (3) = the materials or ingredients necessary

put the final touches on (8) = complete construction of

open up to (10) = give access to

take root in (18) = become established in

ties to (18) = connections with

make it to (20) = reach a place or goal

out of reach (22) = beyond one's ability to do

Answer these questions.

1.   In paragraph 8, what will the French do after they *put the final touches on* the Paris field?
2.   In paragraph 10, when did Italy *open up to* outside influences?
3.   In paragraph 20, have any European players *made it to* the U.S. major leagues?
4.   In paragraph 22, why are the Olympics *out of reach* to most European baseball teams?

IV. Making Sense of Sentences

1.   Paragraph 12 gives three reasons why baseball has become popular in the Netherlands. Two of the reasons are introduced by the word *because*. List the two reasons.

2.   Complete a sentence of your own about baseball.

Baseball (is/is not) popular in my country because _____.

Now reverse the sentence you have written, putting the *because* clause first and a comma after it.

Because _____.

V. Talking and Writing

Discuss the following topics. Then choose one of them to write about.

1.   Most Europeans regard baseball as a hobby. The article makes a distinction between thinking of an activity as a hobby or as a profession. How do you distinguish between these two terms? Do you know someone who has made a hobby into a profession?
2.   Discuss an activity, food or custom that entered your native culture only recently. Where did it come from? How was it popularized?
3.   Have you ever played baseball or watched it being played? How did you like it? Did it remind you of any sport played in your country? What are some similarities?

Sports

Man Still Beats Chess Machine, for Now

Previewing the Article

Sports contests are usually between humans. However, Garri Kasparov, the highest-ranking player in the history of chess, recently took on an unusual opponent. That opponent was Deep Thought, a computer that can examine 720,000 chess positions a second. As the headline indicates, Kasparov won. But how long can humans beat ever more sophisticated computers at this game? Read this article to learn Mr. Kasparov's opinion of his mechanized opponent and the future of humans in chess.

Before You Read

Before you read the article, discuss these questions.
1. Have you ever played chess?
2. Does the idea of playing against a computer in a game interest you? Why, or why not?

As You Read

As you read, notice the specialized vocabulary about chess. You may want to underline or circle new chess words and consult a dictionary if the terms are unfamiliar to you. But you should be able to understand the battle between the computer and the chess champion even if you don't understand all the chess words.

Also, as you read, try to find the differences between the human and the computer in playing the game of chess.

Man Still Beats Chess Machine, for Now

AP/WIDE WORLD PHOTOS

Garri Kasparov, the world chess champion, takes nothing for granted when playing against the computer, Deep Thought.

By Harold C. Schonberg
New York Times Service

NEW YORK—Garri Kasparov, the world chess champion, has played Deep Thought, the world computer chess champion, in a two-game match. He won both games handily, to nobody's surprise, including his own.

Deep Thought recently has been beating grandmasters, including such luminaries as the great Bent Larsen of Denmark, a former contender for the world championship. Does this mean that the era of human chess supremacy is drawing to a close?

Yes, in the opinion of computer and chess experts.

The time is rapidly coming, all believe, when chess computers will be operating with a precision, rapidity and completeness of information that

will far eclipse anything the human mind can do. In three to five years, Deep Thought will be succeeded by a computer with a thousand times its strength and rapidity. And computers scanning a million million positions a second are less than 10 years away.

5   At a news conference, Mr. Kasparov, 26, mildly pointed out that he was, after all, the world champion and the highest-rated player in the history of chess. The International Chess Federation assigns points to players on the basis of the players they beat. Mr. Kasparov beats everybody. His rating has just soared to 2795, which means that he has eclipsed the previous high of 2780, set by Bobby Fischer.

Deep Thought, Mr. Kasparov said, had a strength between 2450 and 2500. How could it beat a player near

2800? He said that he had played many of Deep Thought's games, and that it was possible to steer the computer into lines it did not like or was not prepared for.

"Computers have their psychology too," he said. "If you know a computer well, you can anticipate its moves. Sometimes I can visualize the next move played by a computer."

Mr. Kasparov, unlike many of the experts, was even doubtful that a computer could ever play with the imagination and creativity of a human, though he did look ahead to the next generation of computers and shuddered at what might be coming. Deep Thought can scan 720,000 positions a second. The creators of Deep Thought have developed plans for a machine that can scan a billion positions a second, and it may be ready in five years.

"That means," Mr. Kasparov said with a grin, "that I can be champion for five more years." More seriously, he continued: "But I can't visualize living with the knowledge that a computer is stronger than the human mind. I had to challenge Deep Thought for this match, to protect the human race."

10 Murray Campbell, one of the five scientists who developed Deep Thought, sat before a small console and relayed the computer's moves to the demonstration room.

In a downstairs room, where Mr. Kasparov played, the console, hooked into the mainframe computer at Carnegie-Mellon University, was run by Feng-Hsiung Hsu, another of the scientists. None of the five, incidentally, is a strong chess player.

Before the game, Mr. Campbell had no illusions. Last week, talking about the machine's capabilities, he said that he would be more than happy if it achieved a draw in one of the games.

For his work in the two games Mr. Kasparov's fee was $10,000.

Mr. Kasparov played the black pieces in the first game and went into a Sicilian Defense after the computer's initial move of its king's pawn. He played carefully and precisely, building up a violent attack on the kingside and also developing a passed pawn on the opposite wing. Every chess expert in the room knew after 25 moves or so that Mr. Kasparov had much the better position.

15 But Deep Thought did not agree. When the machine was queried, it kept on insisting that the position was even. Not until about 10 moves before the end did Deep Thought admit that its position was untenable, and that it was playing with the equivalent of a piece down.

After the game Mr. Kasparov said that he never had any doubts, and that his position was superior all the way through. This demonstrated to him how a human mind could exploit the weaknesses of a machine. Deep Thought could analyze any specific

position, he said, but was not much on long-range strategy.

"If a human player was beaten as decisively as I just beat Deep Thought," he said, "he would be so intimidated that he would be an easy target in the second game. But not a machine. It cannot be intimidated."

The second game was not one of Deep Thought's finest two hours. Mr. Kasparov, playing the white pieces, threw moves at it for which it was obviously not programmed. The result was a cramped kingside position for Deep Thought, and Mr. Kasparov moved far ahead in development.

Some in the audience wondered if Mr. Kasparov's remark about a computer's not ever being intimidated was correct. Deep Thought played as though it were frightened of the Soviet grandmaster. Or, said some, Deep Thought was suffering from a virus.

20 After the game Mr. Kasparov was asked what he thought of his electronic opponent. "I was puzzled," he said, "because there was no opposition."

I. Getting the Message

A. After reading the article, choose the best answer for each item.

1. This article is mainly about
   a. the limitations of computers
   b. chess championships
   c. a chess master's experiences playing a computer

2. Within 10 years, computers designed to play chess will
   a. beat Garri Kasparov
   b. scan a million million positions a second
   c. play with more emotion

3. Kasparov believes that he can
   a. develop a better computer
   b. predict the moves of the chess computer
   c. learn new moves from the chess computer

4. Deep Thought was designed by
   a. five scientists
   b. Bent Larsen, a former chess champion
   c. five chess experts

5. Deep Thought had trouble
   a. recognizing that it was losing
   b. playing with black pieces
   c. analyzing specific positions

Check your answers with the key on page 170. If you have made mistakes, reread the article to gain a better understanding of it.

B. Which phrases describe Kasparov and which describe the computer Deep Thought? Put a check (✔) in the correct column.

	Kasparov	Deep Thought
1. can analyze more positions more quickly		
2. can better analyze long-range strategy		
3. cannot recognize being in a bad position very quickly		
4. can control the game by using moves the other was not prepared for		

II. Expanding Your Vocabulary

Getting Meaning from Context

Use context clues to determine the meaning of each word, found in the paragraph(s) indicated in parentheses. Choose the correct definition.

1. handily (1):
   a. easily
   b. using one's hands
2. luminaries (2):
   a. things that give off light
   b. famous people
3. supremacy (2):
   a. dominance
   b. height
4. eclipse (4, 5):
   a. remove light from
   b. surpass
5. shuddered (8):
   a. closed off any thought of
   b. trembled with fear
6. console (10):
   a. a panel with electrical controls
   b. a radio
7. queried (15):
   a. teased
   b. questioned
8. untenable (15):
   a. unable to be supported, weak
   b. soft
9. exploit (16):
   a. take money from
   b. take advantage of
10. intimidated (18):
    a. frightened
    b. slowed

III. Working with Idioms

Study the meanings of these idioms and expressions.

draw to a close (2) = end

be succeeded by (4) = be replaced by

look ahead to (8) = anticipate, look forward to

be run by (11) = be operated by

achieve a draw (12) = tie in a competition

all the way through (16) = from beginning to end

easy target (17) = one easy to defeat

be suffering from (19) = be ill with, be at a disadvantage because of

virus (19) = a disease, here a program that can harm the way a computer runs

Answer these questions.

1. In paragraph 2, why might the era of human chess supremacy be *drawing to a close*?
2. In paragraph 8, why does Mr. Kasparov *look ahead to* the next generation of chess computers with fear?
3. In paragraph 11, was the chess computer *run by* chess experts?
4. In paragraph 12, why did the scientists hope the computer would *achieve a draw* when it played Mr. Kasparov?
5. In paragraph 19, why did some spectators wonder if Deep Thought was *suffering from* a *virus*?

IV. Making Sense of Sentences

In each sentence below, a pronoun is used to refer to a noun or nouns. Find the noun or nouns that relate to each underlined pronoun.

1. The International Chess Federation assigns points to players on the basis of the other players <u>they</u> beat.
2. It was possible to steer the computer into lines <u>it</u> did not like.
3. The creators of Deep Thought have developed plans for a machine that can scan a billion positions a second, and <u>it</u> may be ready in five years.
4. If a human player was beaten as decisively as I just beat Deep Thought, he would be so intimidated that <u>he</u> would be an easy target.

Complete the sentences, using information from the article. For any pronouns you use, indicate the noun that the pronoun refers to.

1. The computer scientists hoped that Deep Thought would do well, but _____.
2. Kasparov challenged Deep Thought because _____.
3. At the end, Kasparov's opinion of Deep Thought was that _____.

V. Talking and Writing

Discuss the following topics. Then choose one of them to write about.

1. Many people have grown accustomed to working with computers in business, education or everyday life. If you operate a computer, when do you find it most useful? Can you see new applications for a computer in your life?
2. Some people foresee dangers from the widespread use of new computer technology. They suggest that computers may interfere with privacy or cause complications in everyday life. Discuss the possible negative effects of computers.
3. If you have ever played chess, pretend you are involved in a game with Deep Thought. Explain your strategy. Did you win or lose?

Sports

Downhill Racers: Taking On the Mountain at Any Risk

Previewing the Article

Courage and confidence are the necessary ingredients when downhill ski racers "take on," or challenge, the mountain course. In this article, Canadian, American and Austrian skiers discuss their motivation for participating in a sport that offers dangers but at the same time not much possibility for most skiers to make large sums of money. As you read the article, decide for yourself whether you believe the personal satisfactions outweigh the risks.

Before You Read

Before you read the article, discuss these questions.
1. What do you think motivates people to engage in risky activities such as downhill skiing, mountain climbing or parachute jumping?
2. Would you be interested in engaging in such an activity? Why, or why not?

As You Read

As you read, look for answers to these questions.
1. Why do some people see downhill ski racing as a glamorous sport?
2. Do participants agree that it is a glamorous sport?

Downhill Racers: Taking On the Mountain at Any Risk

By Nick Stout
International Herald Tribune

VAL D'ISERE, France—If there really is "glamour" in downhill ski racing it is probably because sports enthusiasts, as much as readers and writers of great literature, are forever attracted by the notion of man confronting danger—even death—in pursuit of personal satisfaction.

"It takes a lot of guts to throw yourself down a mountain," Bill Johnson acknowledged proudly after he claimed a gold medal for the United States in the 1984 Olympic Games in Sarajevo, Yugoslavia. "Not many can do that."

More to the point, why would anybody want to?

"It's a really great feeling," Franz Klammer, an Austrian champion, explained recently, looking back on his triumph at the 1976 Olympics in Innsbruck, Austria. "And only a few people can get it. You have to work so hard for so many months. You have to go to the limit."

5 A lasting image of Steve Podborski, who won a bronze medal for Canada in 1980 at Lake Placid, New York, is that of him pumping up his quadriceps in the weightlifting rooms of every hotel on the ski tour. For him, no amount of work was too much for the ultimate payoff.

"Sometimes I'll experience a kind of slow-motion effect," he once said, describing the sensation of a good race. "I'll be going down about 80 or 90 miles an hour and everything will be coming at me quite slowly. You know that you're going fast, but your mind is going slow. That's when you're really on it."

For Klammer, it was something simpler. "It's a feeling of freedom," he said. "Just you and the hill."

Sometimes, of course, the hill wins.

Sep Walcher, one of Klammer's

© V. E. Horne 1992/Unicorn Stock Photos

Downhill racers need courage and confidence. But how glamorous really is their sport?

Austrian teammates, slipped during a race in 1984 and broke his neck. He left a widow and three small children. A year ago, during a training run for the World Cup race on the famous Lauberhorn course in Wengen, Switzerland, a 20-year-old Austrian in his rookie year, Gernot Reinstadler, swerved off the trail at the final gate. Six hours later he died with a broken pelvis and other internal injuries.

10 Success in downhill racing depends on conquering such fears.

Ken Read, the accomplished Canadian whose Olympic memories include a fifth-place finish at Innsbruck, was asked this winter about "the fear factor." Replying slowly, he said: "It governs what you do, but it governs you in a sensible way. Fear is what keeps you from taking unnecessary risks. The difference between winning and losing a race is knowing when to take calculated risks."

What is important, skiers say, is the ability to recognize the difference between fear and nervousness.

"Sometimes I get very nervous," said A. J. Kitt, the leading U.S. downhiller and a credible contender for an Olympic medal in Val d'Isère, "but I don't think I get scared. It's a bad thing to be scared if you're racing downhill because then you hold back a little bit and that's really when a downhiller can get into trouble."

"I try to build my confidence," he continued. "If I'm nervous about a course or a section then I'll take my first training run a little bit easy. Maybe I'll stand up a little earlier than normal in certain sections. Hopefully, by the second or third training run I'll be able to go 100 percent."

15 Confidence, perhaps, is second only to courage in the formula for success in this sport. When Johnson won the Olympic downhill in 1984, people accused him of arrogance when he boasted that he had expected to win. Now doing promotional work for the Crested Butte Mountain Resort in Colorado, Johnson says that he had not meant to be cocky. He really did think he was going to win.

"Even when I was 8 years old," he said, "I knew that if I stayed at it, someday I'd be the best. I knew I had the talent. So what I said wasn't new in Sarajevo. I had been saying it all along."

But confidence can fade fast, as Johnson well remembers. Talking about a training run in 1986, he recalled: "There was a split second of indecision. And I knew then that my days were numbered. My concentration had flipped for a tenth of a second."

As for glamour, Johnson remembered the excitement of Lake Placid in 1980, when, at 19, he was only a forerunner, one of the noncompetitors who ski down the course to pack the snow just before the race. "There was a crowd of 40,000 lining the course from top to bottom," he said, recalling his excitement. He knew then, he said, that his day would come.

There is more to downhill racing than a two-minute Olympic stint every four years, however, and for all its appeal, few skiers would describe their sport as glamorous.

20 "There is no glamour in it at all," Read said when he was one of the top attractions of the World Cup. "In fact, it's very unglamorous. Knowing people from other sports, I'd say we work much harder in training and other things. And the actual competition is much more trying. We go on tour and we work hard. We don't go to the discos and meet all kinds of flashy people. And, contrary to popular opinion, there aren't all sorts of groupies following us."

It is perhaps significant that Johnson's gold medal did little to attract more young Americans into the sport. "Americans see it as a dangerous sport," Johnson said, "and one without many rewards. Parents are more likely to steer their kids into baseball or basketball, where the guys are making seven figures. Money is the major motivation."

Among those who did not need any financial incentive was Dave Irwin, a Canadian who lost control in the Lauberhorn race in January 1976 and subsequently bounced down the course like a rubber ball. Read, who witnessed the accident, had alerted the coaches by walkie-talkie: "Skis and equipment destroyed, blood-filled goggles."

Irwin's 120-kilometer-an-hour (74-mile-per-hour) mistake left him with a severe concussion and fractured rib. Yet, less than a month later, he defied his doctors and sped confidently down the Olympic slope at Innsbruck. He finished respectably, in eighth place, 1.28 seconds behind Klammer.

Months afterward, in a booklet titled, "Ski the Canadian Way," Irwin wrote: "Inside, I feel that there is something tremendously important about the pursuit of fractions of seconds and the challenge of the mountain, even if it means risking so much."

I. Getting the Message

A. After reading the article, choose the best answer for each item.

1. This article is mainly about
    a. current downhill ski champions
    b. how to become a downhill skier
    c. the dangers and rewards of downhill ski racing

2. A typical speed in a downhill ski race is
    a. 60 miles an hour
    b. 120 miles an hour
    c. 80 to 90 miles an hour

3. When the author states that "the hill wins," he means that
   a. the course is difficult
   b. deaths occur
   c. a skier cannot reach a certain speed

4. Fear, Canadian Ken Read believes, keeps a skier from
   a. succeeding at the highest level
   b. appearing arrogant
   c. taking unnecessary risks

5. Champion skier Bill Johnson believes that parents discourage their children from becoming downhill skiers
   a. because of the lack of popularity of the sport
   b. because of the rigorous training
   c. because of the small financial rewards

Check your answers with the key on page 170. If you have made mistakes, reread the article to gain a better understanding of it.

B. List two positive and two negative aspects of downhill skiing.

II. Expanding Your Vocabulary

Getting Meaning from Context

Use context clues to determine the meaning of each word, found in the paragraph indicated in parentheses. Choose the correct definition.

1. enthusiasts (1):   a. people very interested in an activity   b. champions

2. payoff (5):   a. money received   b. reward

3. sensation (6):   a. feeling   b. a dramatic news event

4. accomplished (11):   a. successful   b. skilled

5. contender (12):   a. a possible winner   b. finalist in a contest

6. boasted (14):   a. praised one's own accomplishments   b. lied

7. flashy (20):   a. shiny   b. showy

8. incentive (22):   a. risk   b. motivation

9. defied (23):   a. challenged in a competition   b. disobeyed the advice of

---

III. Working with Idioms

Study the meanings of these idioms and expressions.

take on (headline) = oppose in a competition, challenge

at any risk (headline) = no matter what the danger

a lot of guts (2) = courage

look back on (4) = recall, remember

go the limit (4) = take a risk, not try to be cautious

be on it (6) = be performing, working at one's very best

take a risk (11) = try something dangerous

hold back a little (12) = not fully involve oneself, try to act more carefully

his days were numbered (17) = his time was almost up

his day would come (18) = he'd succeed in the future

groupie (20) = a fan of rock stars or other performers who follows them wherever they perform

left him with (23) = resulted in, caused him to have

Answer these questions.

1. In the headline, what is the extent of danger suggested by the phrase *at any risk*?
2. In paragraph 4, what Olympic victory is Austrian skier Franz Klammer *looking back on*?
3. In paragraph 17, when did Bill Johnson know that *his days* in skiing *were numbered*?
4. In paragraph 18, what experience made the same skier think that *his day would come*?
5. In paragraph 23, what injuries was skier Dave Irwin *left with*?

 IV. Focusing on Style and Tone

Because of the risky nature of downhill skiing, the author includes many colorful phrases to express the dangerous nature of the sport. In paragraph 2, for instance, Bill Johnson speaks of "throw[ing] yourself down a mountain." In paragraph 22, skier Dave Irwin "bounced down the course like a rubber ball." Scan the article for other examples of phrases that vividly express the risks or rewards of downhill skiing. List two of them.

 V. Talking and Writing

Discuss the following topics. Then choose one of them to write about.

1. Of the following list of sports, classify them from most to least dangerous:
   football   boxing   downhill skiing
   baseball   wrestling   race car driving
   basketball   soccer   sky diving

   Put a *G* after the sports that you also believe to be glamorous. Are the more or less dangerous sports glamorous, or does this vary? Compare your answers with those of your classmates.

2. Although downhill skiing is a dangerous sport that tests one's courage, many champion skiers do not see it as a glamorous occupation. Do you believe that it is? What makes a pursuit glamorous? Is money always associated with glamour?

3. Spectators are often attracted to scenes of danger and disaster. Crowds gather to watch fires or performers attempt daring feats like jumping motorcycles over flaming obstacles. Why are people attracted to viewing danger and disaster?

4. Have you ever done or witnessed something dangerous? How did you feel?

FOCUS ON THE NEWSPAPER

Sports

Analyzing Types of Sports Articles; Studying Sports Vocabulary

Who won the Monte Carlo road rally? What teams will be the strongest in the next World Cup soccer tournament? Currently who is the world's fastest human? Most newspapers have sports pages or a sports section that appears daily to answer questions like these.

Contents of Sports Articles

Much of the information on the sports pages is transitory: it is of interest for the current day and may be of little interest the following day. It includes the results of yesterday's games and the prospects for tomorrow's games. But sports feature articles do tackle larger issues, such as the role of business and politics in sports. Other feature articles give insight into the sport itself or into the people who play the sport.

Exercise 1: Who's the Winner?

Choose two or three articles from the sports pages or the sports section and analyze their contents.

Analysis of a Sports Article

1. What is the sport? _____
2. What's the headline? What key words helped you predict the content of the article? _____
3. Is there a photo accompanying the article? If so, what does it show? _____
   _____
4. What is the purpose of the article? Does it report the results of a contest or analyze one about to take place? Or is it a feature article? _____
   _____

For Articles on Sports Results

1. What is the contest? _____
2. Where and when did the event take place? _____
3. Was there a key play or player? _____
4. Is the event discussed in strict chronological order or by highlighting the major events? _____

For Articles on Future Sports Events

1. What is the contest? _____

2. Where and when will the event take place? _____

3. What are the predictions for the outcome? _____

4. What is the importance of the contest? _____

For Sports Feature Articles

1. What is the topic of the article? _____

2. Does the article address issues other than sports (for example, finances, health and so on)? If so, which ones? _____

For Profiles of Sports Figures

1. Why did the newspaper run a feature on this person or team at this time? _____

   _____

2. Did the article portray this person or team sympathetically or unsympathetically?

   _____

3. What sentences gave you the best clues? _____

   _____

4. Did the article make you want to read more about this subject? Why, or why not?

   _____

Exercise 2: The Language of Sports

Each sport has its own terminology. Pick a sport that you know or like.
Look at several newspaper articles reporting the sport. Make a list of basic
terms relating to the sport. Here are some categories into which you can
arrange the terms. Add any additional ones you find.

Positions on the Field	
Plays	
Action Words/Verbs Related to the Sport	
Slang Related to the Sport	
Other	

Share your list with others in the class. Compare your list with those of
other students who chose the same sport.

Comprehension Check

News: Article 1
(page 7)
1. b
2. c
3. c
4. a
5. b

News: Article 2
(page 11)
1. b
2. b
3. c
4. a
5. c

News: Article 3
(page 15)
1. T
2. F
3. T
4. F
5. T
6. T
7. F

News: Article 4
(page 20)
1. b
2. c
3. c
4. a
5. b

Opinion: Article 1
(page 28)
1. c
2. c
3. b
4. a
5. b

Opinion: Article 2
(page 31)
1. c
2. c
3. a
4. b
5. a

Opinion: Article 3
(page 36)
1. a
2. c
3. a
4. b

Opinion: Article 4
(page 41)
1. b
2. c
3. c
4. c
5. a
6. b

Opinion: Article 5
(page 46)
1. F
2. T
3. T
4. T
5. F
6. F
7. T

Business: Article 1
(page 54)
1. c
2. b
3. a
4. b
5. c

Business: Article 2
(page 59)
1. T
2. F
3. F
4. T
5. T
6. F

Business: Article 3
(page 64)
1. T
2. F
3. F
4. F
5. T
6. T
7. T
8. T

Business: Article 4
(page 70)
1. a
2. c
3. b
4. c
5. a

Education: Article 1
(page 78)
1. c
2. a
3. a
4. b

Education: Article 2
(page 83)
1. F
2. T
3. F
4. T
5. T
6. F
7. T

Education: Article 3
(page 88)
1. c
2. b
3. c
4. a
5. b

Education: Article 4
(page 93)
1. T
2. T
3. F
4. T
5. T
6. F

Arts and Leisure: Article 1
(page 101)
1. b
2. b
3. c
4. a

Arts and Leisure: Article 2
(page 105)
1. b
2. b
3. a
4. b
5. c
6. c
7. c

Arts and Leisure: Article 3
(page 110)
1. F
2. F
3. T
4. T

Arts and Leisure: Article 4
(page 117)
1. F
2. T
3. T
4. F
5. F
6. T

**Arts and Leisure: Article 4,
Follow-up Article**
(page 120)
1. Going Down
2. Going Down
3. Not Discussed
4. Going Up
5. Not Discussed
6. Going Down

Science and Environment: Article 1
(page 126)
1. b
2. b
3. c
4. a
5. a

Science and Environment: Article 2
(page 131)
1. b
2. c
3. b
4. b
5. b
6. c

Science and Environment: Article 3
(page 136)
1. a
2. b
3. b
4. c
5. a

Science and Environment: Article 4
(page 142)
1. F
2. T
3. F
4. T
5. T
6. T
7. F
8. T

Sports: Article 1
(Page 149)
1. c
2. a
3. c
4. b
5. b
6. b

Sports: Article 2
(page 155)
1. F
2. F
3. T
4. F
5. F
6. T

Sports: Article 3
(page 159)
1. c
2. b
3. b
4. a
5. a

Sports: Article 4
(page 164)
1. c
2. a
3. b
4. c
5. c